The Gift of
INNER HEALING

Ruth Carter Stapleton

WORD BOOKS, PUBLISHER
Waco, Texas

First Printing—February 1976
Second Printing—April 1976
Third Printing—June 1976
Fourth Printing—June 1976
Fifth Printing—June 1976
Sixth Printing—September 1976

THE GIFT OF INNER HEALING

ISBN 0-87680-449-0

Library of Congress catalog card number: 75–36180
Printed in the United States of America

Quotations from the Revised Standard Version of the Bible, copyright 1946 (renewed 1973), 1956 and (c) 1971 by the Division of Christian Education of the National Council of the Churches of Christ in the United States of America, used by permission; *The New English Bible* © The Delegates of The Oxford University Press and The Syndics of The Cambridge University Press, 1961, 1970, reprinted by permission; *The New Testament in Modern English* by J. B. Phillips, © J. B. Phillips 1958, 1960, 1972.

To all of those
whose ministry has
helped me unlock doors of
meaning in my own life

CONTENTS

INTRODUCTION

When we speak of inner healing, we refer to the experience in which the Holy Spirit restores health to the deepest area of our lives by dealing with the root cause of our hurts and pain. In prayer for physical healing we are often concerned with the symptoms of the real need. Deep hurts and fears often manifest themselves physically as backaches, headaches, skin rashes, asthma, and other illnesses. When we pray for healing of physical symptoms, we often see no change because we are praying for and expecting God to heal the symptom rather than to make us whole.

We must realize that it is God's will for us to be whole and understand that our Father really desires to heal our attitudes. Frequently our problems are initiated by lack of love and understanding from others rather than by sins we have committed.

Since Jesus Christ is the same yesterday, today, and tomorrow, he is able to go back into our lives and heal the traumatic episodes. Very often we have suppressed the hurtful occurrences so completely that we are not even aware of their bind upon our hearts. If we let him, the Holy Spirit, who reveals all things, is able to bring to our awareness the situations which need our attention. Since the Holy Spirit is a gentleman, he will never overcome our free will but will wait patiently for us to invite him to enter. "Behold, I stand at the door" until you are ready to open it to me.

In the Old Testament God says: "I will sprinkle clean water upon you, and you shall be clean . . . a new heart I will give you, and a new spirit I will put within you; and I will take out of your flesh the heart of stone and give you a heart of flesh . . . I will set you free."

Some areas within our lives can only be healed by the power of the Holy Spirit. Psychiatrists bring a degree of healing by probing into the past and bringing understanding of our weak and vulnerable spots and our angry and fearful reactions, but only the Holy Spirit can move back into these areas and remove the scars.

When we pray for inner healing, we are really asking Jesus to walk back into the dark places of our lives and bring healing to the distressing and painful memories of the past. We need to take Jesus into the areas of our unforgiveness toward these who have taught us to fear, hate, and reject. We need to take him (love) into the relationships where there was no love.

As we respond to prayer by imagining Jesus moving back into our lives, we picture the little child within us who hurts, who was rejected, who failed to receive healthy love, who was neglected by the parents' failure to give corrective discipline in love, and who wasn't understood. That little child within each of us must harken to the healing love of Jesus Christ. We then need the help of another person to prepare the way for our hearts to be opened.

Sometimes we need to reach out to others who are blocked and bound. The law of the Spirit is, "As you give, so shall you receive." Many who have been frustrated in their desire to be healed through prayer and conscious effort find their own healing when they reach out to others.

Love is the key to open the heart, the love that St. Paul said, "Bears all things, believes all things, hopes all things, endures all things" (1 Cor. 13:7). This Christ-like love opens the heart to Jesus Christ. He is the only one who can speak to our deepest needs and bring total healing to every man.

1

THE PROCESS
OF INNER HEALING

"I have come that men may have life, and may have it in all its fullness" (John 10:10, NEB*).*

"Ruth, you wanted to die!" I sat in the library at my home listening to words I didn't want to hear but which I knew were true. It all seemed like a terrible nightmare—the hundred different pressures within, the disappointments and failures without.

Until the friend seated across from me said that I wanted to die, it just seemed like an awful accident. I knew nothing about "accident proneness" or the "will to die." I certainly didn't think that my dedicated Christian life was being threatened by memories I couldn't recall—until yesterday morning.

I was driving away from my home down the gradually sloping street that winds through our lovely subdivision in one of the "nicer" parts of Fayetteville, North Carolina. When I pressed on the brake, the peddle went to the floorboard. "No brakes!" I screamed inside. I can't remember just what happened. But before I could think—or did I want to think?—I opened the door and threw myself out of the car. As the car crashed into a power pole, I lay on the pavement, badly cut and bleeding, dazed, but in one piece. All around me stretched live wires that had been torn from the pole by the collision, but none touched me.

As my friend began to question me about my childhood, I felt both frightened and encouraged. He suggested that Jesus Christ could walk into the graveyard of my past pains, where I had buried alive so many experiences, resurrect them, and change the ugliness that haunted and drove me uncontrollably into beautiful memories and healthy patterns of behavior that would bless me forever. Too good to be true? Well, I thought so. But like many who have hit rock bottom, I had nowhere else to go. I had to find healing. I really didn't want to live, though on the surface, it seemed that I had everything to live for.

My friend offered to pray for the "healing of the memories." I didn't understand what he meant. My life had been lived in prayer. His proposal could be one more of those too-good-to-be-true "solutions" that solve nothing. Many people run from one method to another that promises peace and happiness. It's easy to be conned when you're hurt. But I didn't have anything to lose; so I gave it a try.

What I experienced began to bring stability to my life. I learned that inner healing is a process, not a moment. It is, in fact, a means of accelerating the emotional growth that is the natural product of following the person and words of Jesus Christ. The only thing it provides that is usually lacking in the average "good Christian's" life is deep insight into what makes us do what we know is wrong and not do what we know is right. St. Paul described our frustration: "For I find myself not doing what I really want to do but doing what I really loathe" (Rom. 7:15, Phillips). Healing of the memories allows us to deal cleanly and precisely with the root problems; it is one means of instilling positive images deep in the mind. I learned that those images greatly determine how we respond to each moment in life.

I became angry, but I found that anger was not my problem. Rejection was. I would become bitter toward others, some who were dearest to me. I didn't see the reason for that bitterness and anger until I looked back into my childhood. As I related to some people, I was unconsciously expecting what I had experienced as a child—love to a point and then what felt like rejection.

I first became aware of my rejection feelings when I married at the age of nineteen. To that point my emotions were pretty "normal," but the problem was there, buried inside me. When I moved into the demanding adult relationship of marriage, I found myself terrifyingly unprepared.

My understanding and healing began with the questions, What was your relationship with your father and mother? What was your childhood like?

My father had been dead for seventeen years, and I remembered him as the most wonderful, the most beautiful man I had ever known in my life . . . in fact, the only perfect human being.

"He adored me," I told my inquiring friend. "He worshiped the ground I walked on." That was my friend's first clue that all had not been right in my father-daughter relationship.

I further explained that my mother is just great. "We have so much fun together; she's fantastic."

Everything seemed positive, too positive.

As I shared my childhood memories and recent crises, I found that the little girl of my childhood had not always felt so positively. I discovered hidden resentment toward my parents. After prayer and a "guided meditation," I experienced why the Bible says that the Holy Spirit is "the revealer of the secrets of the heart." I began to see my childhood in a new and healing light. First, I realized that much of what I thought was my parents' perfection was at the heart of my problem.

My father had loved me very deeply, but his way of expressing that love was not altogether healthy. He had given me everything I had ever wanted. "Ruth," he used to tell me, "you are the most wonderful person in the world."

I had been raised to believe that I was God's gift to the world, the most beautiful child ever born. I was led to believe that I was the most talented, the most gifted of persons. I grew up thinking I was queen of the universe.

Because of my sheltered and protected life, I never really learned about the outside world. Because my father did not want me to be hurt, I was protected from many experiences that would cause suffering or pain. Although I lived on a farm in south Georgia, I never saw an animal born. Relatives passed away, but I was spared the pain of ever attending the funeral. I never had to endure the creative but often painful conflict of making a decision of any importance.

My mother didn't indulge me as my father did. She treated all the children alike. This registered on my emotions as rejection. So in marriage I was trapped in what seemed to be a cold, cruel world. I expected rejection and found it. I wanted to flee into the unrealistic existence of my childhood and couldn't.

At home I had played with the black children on the farm. I never knew until I became an adult that there had been an unwritten law, spawned by centuries of prejudice, that the white children must be allowed to win all the time. So every game I ever played throughout my entire childhood, I won. I was best at kick-the-can, fastest in any race, and I always caught my friends immediately at hide-and-seek. I grew up believing that I was the most gifted, most loved person in the world.

When I went away to college and later when I married, I was shocked to discover an inability to cope normally with life. I was not the best, the most beautiful, the most loved of all. I didn't have all the answers, and I was almost totally unable to make decisions. Because I was unable to face my inadequacies, I had to blame other people and circumstances. I constantly fell into states of depressions and anxiety which led to hypertension. I couldn't have described my feelings in such clinical terms; I just wanted to scream. When one who has been conditioned to believe that love and being "center stage" are synonymous doesn't get one's way, the reaction is to feel totally rejected. Every time one's preference is not forthcoming, that experience comes across as rejection. To fall short of "number one" in any area of life registers as unbearable failure. Life becomes a trap—rejection and failure everywhere, no place to hide.

After moving four hundred fifty miles from my family in order to save my marriage, I found myself in a cold, threatening, unprotected world, or so it seemed to my confused heart. In an effort to avoid total destruction, I indulged in escapes of every kind (art lessons, piano lessons, photography lessons, childhood fantasies, and membership in every available club).

A major crisis arose when I discovered I was pregnant with my first child. I knew that this was supposed to be one of the crowning moments of womanhood, but not for me. No one knew how I trembled inside. I was not prepared to deal with such responsibilities. When my baby was born, I wanted to be a good mother, but I felt even more trapped. I felt like such a failure. Bottles and diapers were hard enough. I knew the care and comfort my baby needed, but I felt as much need for this as that darling baby I was sometimes afraid to hold. Then three more babies were born in rapid succession, and each one, so beautiful, terrified me. I did love them, but by the fourth child I was at the point of total desperation. I no longer had the illusion of being queen of the universe. Now I was gripped with the illusion that I was a hopeless failure—as a wife, as a mother, as a person.

During this dark period I found a living faith in God. Jesus Christ became my life, and I surrendered control of my troubled existence to the Spirit. (I was happy to let

go.) This experience began the healing process. I had a
new life just as Jesus promised. It was no warmed-over
theology; I knew the love of Christ. I saw the miracle of
his love heal the sick, restore broken lives, inspire one to
selfless service. For the first time in my adult life I experienced hope and joy that allowed me to begin to live. I
thought my problems had ended and that I was to have joy
and peace forever.

How shocked I was to find myself struggling with the
same old weaknesses. A friend in whom I had put all my
trust crushed me with what seemed like heartless cruelty.
I was hit at my point of greatest vulnerability, rejection.
In desperation I reached out for help. The religious would
say, "I'll pray about it." The nonreligious would imply
regret and murmur, "Well, that sort of thing happens."
But I found no help. Desolate, I agonized in prayer. Where
was Jesus? "Is there no help?" I cried.

I wanted to forgive, but I couldn't. And this crisis
deepened as I began to see in my life one area of emotional and spiritual failure after another. It was like trying to sweep back an ocean tide with a broom. So many
things were right. I had a lovely home, security, fine children, a husband who was such a good man with a real
commitment to Jesus Christ. But something was danger-
ously wrong. When I had begun my Christian life, I learned
that Jesus said that I must be last and least. My father
had taught me that I was first and best. I began to realize
that this was why it was so hard for me to "work out my
salvation," to become a whole, stable person. At this point
I jumped out of my car.

Over a period of months the man who prayed for the healing of my deep mind, that region which carefully records and stores every experience of life, led me back behind the locked doors of my memory. I began to see the root of jealousies and hates that tortured me and hurt and disappointed others. Seeing the problem was not healing in itself, but understanding is the light that precedes the day of healing if one wills to be healed.

I began to feel angers toward my parents I had never allowed to surface. It was important that those angers did come up, that I did face them, but clearly there is a deeper level of understanding. Anger is a valid emotion, usually prostituted by the ego. Someone, we feel, hurts us; so we get mad. In therapy some glorify this selfish anger and call it honesty. But as I went deeper into myself, I realized that blaming others is not honest but immature. It was where I was, and I am grateful to those who accepted my anger and thus showed me I was accepted. But the day came in my healing, which continues, when I knew that I couldn't blame my parents or others. I can see where they failed, accept them unconditionally, and allow the Holy Spirit to "restore the harvest the locusts have destroyed." Which is just what happened.

Each person's story is different from mine, yet the same. Our childhood began to build into our memory banks assets and liabilities from which we draw every day of our lives. We enjoy life where we are emotionally blessed and tend to ignore where we are poor or bankrupt until some life situation makes us look at the ledger and we begin to see our dilemma. These crisis moments that seem so unbearable, the stale periods when the diversion and entertainments don't ease, are good. The emptiness and the ache are God's dark angels. Such negative moments are messengers telling us that there are places in our past which need healing.

The experience of inner healing begins when some circumstance such as a spiritual experience, an insight created by some healing method applied either psychologically or spiritually, or the will to be whole occurs. Of course this last factor, the will to be whole, lies behind every experience of healing. When in the depths of seeming hopelessness one wills wholeness, he or she can begin to draw .ll that is needed for healing. The economy of the universe .s built on love and operates on will. It doesn't matter what I feel; what I will to experience is what will finally be. That gives hope to anybody, even those experiencing the greatest darkness or despair life can create. The God of love made the first step to wholeness so totally available to the most broken life—the will to be made whole.

When my "hot house" roof fell in on this oversheltered plant, I had no psychological knowledge or spiritual support. But I wanted to be well; I did will to be whole. That is about all I had going for me, but realistically, at that awful point, it was enough.

What led to my spiritual experience, my first step into life worth living, was an invitation to a nonsectarian Christ-centered camp the summer after my fourth baby was born. I had never known of this camp or of these people, but among them I found unconditional love. They unselfconsciously led me to an experience of God, a loving, caring, personal God, and a Jesus Christ that I had never known in my life as a church member. He was living; he was here and now. That literally saved my life.

Because as a child of God I willed to be whole, it was inevitable, predictable, that I would meet, step by step, the ghosts of the past, so that they could be removed forever from my life.

The friend who led me into my first experience of the healing of memories once said, "God will do everything you cannot do in order that you may live; he will do nothing that you can do in order that you may grow."

This is vital. The life of your mind is a wonderful and mysterious part of the universe. Anyone who claims to understand it knows nothing of its depth. God can restore the mind to life; we can't, any more than we can create new brain tissue. But where there is that sense of life which the Love of Jesus Christ brings, we can give ourself to the task of cutting out the old sick memories and replacing them with new rich images in our deep mind. These new images lead to whole, constructive living. Removing old material and replacing it with the new is the total objective of the healing of the memories.

2

THE CHILD,
REVEALED AND HEALED

"Suffer the little children to come unto me, and forbid them not: for of such is the kingdom of God" (Mark 10:14, KJV).

Mary Ann admitted that her marriage was miserable. She loved her children. She said it was worth the pain of her marital difficulties just to be their mother. She loved her husband too, but why were things with him going down the drain? The sweet, young housewife, mother of three, was sitting to my left. Her fashionable beige and white suit was carefree, but her face betrayed deep tensions.

She nodded as I suggested that at the beginning of the love relationship we usually relate to a fiancé on the conscious level. After marriage, a spouse often becomes irritating or even a total disappointment. Then we say, "The honeymoon is over." What is really happening is that the inner child who lives on the subconscious level has been pacified by the conscious glitter of romantic attention. Afterward, basic feelings begin to surface, and the inner child demands attention.

23

Every inner child has an image of a man and woman formed by his relationship with mother and father. When mother lives a joyous, fulfilling role as a woman and mother, the child within develops a positive female image. If the father is emotionally strong, responsible, and loving, the child forms a positive male image. When either masculine or feminine image breaks down, the child's response to his adult role is affected. If the inner psychic child has been abused, we sometimes find an inner battered-child syndrome. "As a man thinks in his inner-child heart so is he."

Turning to Mary Ann I said, "You may want to try to see what kind of image of a woman, and of a man, you brought into your marriage. But before we get into anything like that, may I pray with all of you for the healing of the inner child in each of us?"

The *all* I referred to was a group of twelve who had one thing in common: firsthand experience of a living faith in Jesus Christ. Close as a group, they had invited me to spend a week of concentrated sharing because they felt they needed help. (They knew that what they had was real enough.) Their informal sharing sessions in each home was a weekly "must," but even after recognizing their patterns, they were still puzzled and troubled about why some personal problems persisted and even grew worse when others didn't.

I began a long prayer which attempted, through the power of the Holy Spirit, to help them relive some of their early memories and to allow some of those early repressed memories to surface.

As we finished the prayer, I looked up. The pharmacist was bent over, holding a handkerchief over his eyes. Body language confessed brokenness. Others were crying too.

As we discussed what had been experienced during the prayer and the silent contemplation which followed, two people said, "Nothing happened."

"That may be, and that's O.K.," I said. "But you may find that later tonight, or tomorrow, a delayed reaction will bring up memories. The healing process often begins with emotion."

Mary Ann, the young mother, spoke up, "A lot came to me."

"Can you share it with the group?" I asked.

"Certainly." She spoke with the warm confidence of someone who trusted this circle of friends. "I was a depression baby, the third of six children. Our family had little money. As you were praying, I realized how deeply I felt like Poor Plain Jane. I resented my mother for dressing me in hand-me-downs and for not giving me the attention I thought I needed. But, gosh, with six kids, what else could she do?" She was smiling but tearful now. "As you prayed, Ruth, mama and I had a real reconciliation tonight. She doesn't know about it yet, but tomorrow I'll call and tell her. For the first time I feel I *want* to call her, instead of calling her out of duty, which I've always done before."

Another lovely, young woman stood up. Mary Ann, anticipating her embrace, stood up too. They moved across the circle into each other's arms in the kind of love and acceptance for which we all hunger.

Sitting down, Mary Ann said, "I have another problem

though. My father was a good man; he was just always busy. I can't remember his showing me affection. I mean putting his arms around me or kissing me. Gosh, I can't even imagine his doing that." She hesitated, "Could this be a problem in my relationship with Nick?"

"Well, yes, it certainly could be," I responded.

"Well, it sounds like nonsense to me," interrupted Clifton. Clifton had reacted negatively from our first meeting. "Why not just pray about it?" he said brashly. "You don't have to be psychoanalyzed, and you don't need a psychiatrist when you have Jesus!"

My first impression of Clifton was "tall, dark, and homely." The shadow of sadness in his demeanor was in deep contrast to the joy-filled Bible that he carried. His words continued, matching the look of disapproval upon his face: "Don't give me all that 'healing-of-the-memories' stuff. I don't need to dig up the past and relive a lot of old experiences."

Even though I had never met Clifton before, he seemed very angry.

"All I need is prayer and the Bible."

Underscore the *prayer*, I thought, and smiling I said, "If what I'm saying disturbs you, forgive me. But the experiences I'm talking about will only make your Bible and prayer time a deeper, freer experience."

Well, he wasn't convinced, but neither was I intimidated. I knew from a look at my own life that with all the religion I had experienced, I was never really alive until Jesus, in his love, touched those dark and painful memories in *my* past. Even after the authentic and life-changing ex-

26

perience of being "baptized in the Holy Spirit," I had felt periods of great anxiety and frustration until I began to find healing for painful, obstructing childhood memories.

"We both know that prayer is essential," I said, "but there are many different ways to pray. Prayer opens the heart so that we can deal with memories buried in emotion. Christ's love alone can remove these emotional barriers in order that we might be freed to experience the flow of his love.

"Being able to receive his love helps us grow. You know, it's like the blind spot in our eye. Every person has a physical one, and on the mental level is a 'corresponding' blind spot that we are completely unable to see with or into. We must have help, or we will never know what is there. Mentally we are 'blind' to ourselves in certain areas, and the greatness of the love of Jesus Christ is that he can reach in and touch and heal these areas if we are willing . . ."

"Well, it doesn't seem scriptural to me," he growled.

"Can we try to deal with Mary Ann's question now? Then I'd be happy to discuss yours at length."

He smiled. The cliffs were beginning to crumble even if they hadn't yet tumbled. I turned to Mary Ann, looked her full in the face, and then asked:

"Mary Ann, in all honesty, who do you think has been more at fault in your unhappy marriage, you or your husband?"

"Nick," she said without hesitation.

"Is Nick affectionate toward you?"

"He was when we were first married. But never any

27

more. Except when we go to bed. Then he gets all lovey, and I resent it. I feel like he's just using me."

"He may be. But would you be willing to be as much at fault as he is? Possibly without even knowing it? Dr. Missildine, in his book, *Your Inner Child of the Past,* says, 'There are four people in every marriage bed: a man and a woman, and a little boy and a little girl.' What he means is that we bring to marriage our adult selves plus what our childhood has been conditioned to feel."

"I don't quite understand what you're saying." Mary Ann was openly puzzled.

"It took me a long time to understand a little of this myself. But what little I do understand has helped change my life. Tell me now, just be honest—do you want your husband's affection?" I asked.

"Oh, yes!" she exclaimed. "I ache for it."

"But you never expected it from your daddy?"

She paused. "Never."

"Could it be that what you're doing in bed, and out of bed too, is sending two messages to your husband? The adult message is, 'I want your love and affection.' The second is the little girl message, "I don't expect you to love me. I expect you are like my father. I expect you to be distant and unaffectionate.' And your inner rejected child resents this expectation. The unhappy truth might be that the last message is more powerful because it comes from your deep emotions. If this is true, is it any wonder that your husband has turned you off? Can you imagine how he feels when you are verbally saying all the right things, but the message he gets from the subconscious inner child

—from your gut level—is an ugly put-down? Perhaps even he at times doesn't understand why he reacts so violently toward you when you are being so nice on the surface."

"So how do I get my inner child to cooperate?" Mary Ann was approaching the healing point.

"If you want to follow this through to healing, Mary Ann, I want you to go back in your memory, or in your imagination, to the age where you can recall wanting your father's affection, when you remember most deeply the pain of not having it."

She looked down at her high-fashion dress boots while crossing her arms over her stomach. Her body language revealed that my question had figuratively hit her in the stomach. She was trying not to remember a hurt she hadn't allowed herself to feel for years. She didn't want to dredge up those feelings.

"It's hard to say when I felt the need for his love most. I guess when I was eleven, twelve, maybe thirteen. I just really don't remember that well."

"Can you remember an incident during that time?"

"Let's see." We sat in silence as she thought. "I remember when I went to my first dance. I was thirteen. My mother and I had made my first evening gown, and I was really excited. I felt not-so-drab, almost pretty. After I had every hair in place, I walked out into the living room to wait for my date, and daddy was reading the newspaper. Although I don't remember the boy's name or much of anything about that night, I remember I felt for weeks the hurt that daddy didn't say a word about me or my pretty dress. He just kept his head buried in that damned newspaper!"

"That's helpful, Mary Ann. Often it's not that a parent is so terrible. Your father certainly intended no harm. But after many little hurts we begin to suppress them. Then there can be big trouble in the repression of the memories related to hurts. Close your eyes now and go back in your imagination to that living room on the night you described." I silently prayed, "Lord, heal her heart."

"All right, I'm there," she said.

"Do you see your father reading the newspaper?"

"I sure do. I want to tear it out of his hand and say, 'Look at me, daddy!' "

"Before you do anything, Mary Ann, look toward the front door. See it opening. See Jesus walking in."

As quickly as I set the scene she said, "I see him."

"You see Jesus?"

"Yes," she responded quickly. "He walked in and is standing over by the oil stove."

"Let him come over to you and tell you how lovely you look."

"Oh, my soul, what a beautiful man he is."

"Yes, he is. What does he think of you?"

"He says I'm beautiful. He says he's very proud of me, that he would be proud to take me out." Tears were flowing from Mary Ann's eyes. "He kissed me on the forehead."

I'm perpetually awed by how beautifully the Spirit works.

"Now, Mary Ann, let Jesus go over to your father. See a radiant light flow from Jesus into your father."

"Daddy's put the paper down. He's looking up at me."

"If your daddy was flooded with the Spirit of Jesus, what do you think your daddy would do?"

"He'd come and tell me he loves me."

"Let him." Then came that moment of reconciliation and understanding I had seen so many times before, but it is always new, always sacred.

I turned to the pharmacist and said, "Would you kneel before Mary Ann and be her daddy? Say to her what you feel he would say."

He rose, walked to where Mary Ann was seated, and knelt down. He took her two hands in his and said, "Mary Ann, I do love you. I always have. I just didn't know how to express it. Please forgive me."

The pharmacist's words were stilted, rigid. I detected fear in him. Because members of a group such as this, dedicated to the Holy Spirit, become mystically related to each other, because they become an organic microcosm of the Body of Christ, frequently when one attempts, in the Spirit of Love, to help another, his own needs begin to be revealed, then met.

But Mary Ann, in her creative faith imagination, was psychically standing before her father, not the pharmacist. She heard her father's words, felt the touch of her father's hands, and saw "the evidence of things not seen"—her father asking her to forgive him.

"Daddy, I forgive you," Mary Ann said through her tears. "I know you didn't know, but I just couldn't help how I cheated I felt."

The pharmacist was afraid to go any further. He knelt

awkwardly, obviously not wanting to dare the indicated paternal embrace.

So I said to Mary Ann, "Just see your daddy embracing you and telling you how lovely you are."

"Oh, yes." She spoke those two words with a sigh of near ecstasy.

While Mary Ann was still emotionally responding to the prayer, I suggested that she imagine her husband, Nick, coming into the room. Then, as she had experienced the forgiveness with her father, I suggested that she forgive Nick and that Nick forgive her.

When the two, the husband and wife, were reconciled in Christ's healing love, I asked the group to join in a circle around Mary Ann.

"Jesus, you promised that whatever we bind on earth will be bound in heaven. We bind this experience of reconciliation of father and husband to Mary Ann's heart. May it bring a new experience of love to her, and into her marriage. Amen."

After the circle of friends had returned to their chairs, I told Mary Ann, "Remember, this is only a crucially important beginning. Your inner child is going to have to build, by daily faith, that strong image of a man you saw tonight in your imagination.

"Try to spend a little time each day visualizing Jesus coming in the door from work. Then see yourself walking up to him, embracing him. Say to Jesus, 'It's good to have you home, Nick.'

"If you do this each day, you will condition yourself to respond to Nick as you would respond to Jesus. Months could go by before you observe any visible results. But each time you do it, you will nourish and strengthen that inner child. *This is the most powerful prayer you can pray for your husband."*

Many experiences in faith-imagination therapy produce good, but unknown, results. But sometimes we get a bonus: we find out. In Mary Ann's case, revelation came nearly a year later. In a church in the East, a most attractive young man in his mid-thirties came up to me.

"You don't know me, Mrs. Stapleton," he said, "but you know my wife, Mary Ann Davis."

"You're Nick!" I said with unguarded enthusiasm.

"You have some kind of memory, Mrs. Stapleton," he smiled.

"Not at all, Nick, no trick to remember Mary Ann. She made quite an impression on me."

"I interrupted a business engagement in the city to come over to thank you," he continued. "I don't know what you said to my wife. I do know that after the week with you in that group her whole attitude toward life seemed to change. Before meeting you, she had reason to be upset: I was running around on her. Afterward she became so tender and understanding. I couldn't handle the freight. She didn't say one word about religion when she came home from that meeting, but I was sure she must have had some sort of religious experience. I really couldn't understand the change in her until after I went with her to a church conference. Christ became real to me for the first time; you might say he became my life. I guess I don't need to tell you that Mary Ann and I have a whole new relationship. Well, all of this is to say, 'Thank you for your part in our new life.' "

Nick seemed to understand when I couldn't say anything. I'm sure he understood my tears. He pressed my hand. We both knew no further words were possible or necessary. He smiled, kissed me on the cheek, and slipped into the crowd.

3

RELEASE FROM A COMMON BONDAGE
TO A PERFECT FREEDOM

"If the Son, then, sets you free, you are really free!" (John 8:36, Phillips).

Turning to Jeff, the young pharmacist, I asked, "How did you feel when you were kneeling before Mary Ann?"

"I was hoping you hadn't noticed," he said.

I smiled, remained silent, waited for him to continue.

"What was I feeling like? I wasn't feeling good, that's for sure. The last time I felt that bad was when I found myself with only a dime in my pocket to pay a restaurant bill of ten dollars."

Was he indulging in evasion through humor? He looked as if he were hoping I'd accept his comic comment as enough.

"How did you feel?" I persisted, gently.

"Ruth, I just plain didn't like getting into Mary Ann's emotions. This bothers me because I feel close to her. We've been in this group since it began. She and I met Christ at the same time."

But Eve, the tall, stately secretary next to Jeff interjected, "Yes, but you sure do lean on her every once in awhile."

There was quiet consensus from most of the others.

In groups such as this, I try to focus my mind upon Jesus in a constant internal prayer. I know Jesus wills the good of his flock, and sometimes when it seems that my will is totally in tune with his—when I too will the ultimate good of another—I receive intuitive insights.[1]

In this moment, I saw Jeff standing before an unknown woman, obviously his mother. There were cords like octopus tentacles coming from her and clinging all over him. I sensed that she had never let him go and that Jeff was still trying to be free. He had a deep hidden dislike for women. But to tell him all that I saw and felt would have been imprudent, if not impertinent. If the insight were true, he would have been unable to accept it from one more manipulating, threatening woman. Obviously, this was the last thing he needed. I decided not to speak of the insight at this time but to put it on "the back burner" and go on.

"Jeff, let's drop the question of how you felt toward Mary Ann. Could you tell us a little about your mother and father?"

"You mean Dr. Jekyll and Mr. Hyde?" he laughed.

"Oh, really? Which was which?"

"I'll start with Mr. Hyde. That was dad. He used a 'wire brush' on me. He was a hard man. Once when I was about five years old I left the barn door open after doing some chores. He erupted like a volcano. It was getting late and darkness was closing in when he let me have it. He hit me a couple of open-handed haymakers and told me to 'get out there and close that barn door!' I took off running just to get away from him, but when I stepped out on the porch into that dark, I was scared out of my wits. The trip down to that barn door and back seemed like a hundred miles. That's one of the fond memories of my old man. My mother was my protector."

With Jeff, as with most of us, the circumstances of his childhood were not quite as he saw them, either through five-year-old eyes or in retrospect. Sometimes when we think one parent is responsible for most of our pain, and that the other is innocent, we later learn that the seemingly innocent one has caused the problem. Repressed memories sometime give more trouble than clear memories. If we are consciously aware that our faults have been caused by someone, we can usually deal with them, but those forgotten, or those unseen, can be blocks that we must struggle to uncover and deal with.

I became intuitively sure that Jeff, in blaming his father and glorifying his mother, was wrong. His deepest problems were repressed memories originating from his mother.

"Mother always stood up for me. We had a good thing going until I got engaged. I don't know what went wrong, but she got bitter, turned on me, and almost succeeded in breaking up my fiancée and me. She felt it would be a poor marriage. I guess she was right; Marceen and I didn't last six years. Mother calls me and visits pretty often, but it's never been quite the same. I feel guilty about how it's been, but mother and I can't seem to get into the swing of our old relationship. It really puzzles me." He went on to "Mr. Hyde."

"The relationship with dad has been pretty well taken care of. After I became a Christian, he was the first person I went to. We cried buckets together. A real wet reunion, just eleven months before he died. I walked away from that experience saying to Jesus, 'Dear Heavenly Brother, if you never do another thing for me, thank you forever.' And, Ruth, I was crying the same way when you prayed that prayer of forgiveness for the group. I relived some of the pain of my hate toward him that I thought was completely gone. The healing that was begun on that great day when dad and I went into each other's arms in real love has now been completed."

"Jeff, if you relived some of that pain with dad, then it's not completely gone or completely healed. What memory occurred that caused the tears just now?"

"Fear of the dark! Fear of that long journey—as a five-year-old—to that barn to lock the door."

"Jeff, close your eyes. Your father has just roared at you, hit you, as you said, with two 'open-handed haymakers.' Do you see this?"

Eyes shut, he trembled convulsively.

"Now, Jeff, *before* you go outside into the dark, imagine that just outside that door Jesus is waiting for you. Before you go out, do you see him there, just outside?"

"I do."

"Do you see him waiting to catch you up into his arms and hold you to his chest?"

"I do."

"All right. Now, Jeff, go out that door into the dark where Jesus is waiting . . ."

"I have . . . and Jesus has caught me up into his arms."

"And they're so strong, Jeff, that you feel his tremendous strength and energy and power flowing into you. Now nothing in the world can harm you. There's nothing at all to be afraid of. Do you feel his strength coming into you?"

"Oh, I do, Ruth. I've never felt so strong and—and fearless."

"All right. Now, Jeff, Jesus is going to put you down—right outside the door—and you, a five-year-old boy, are going to hold Jesus' hand. Together you two, hand in hand, are going to walk through the dark, step by step, to that barn door. Has Jesus put you down on the ground?"

"Yes."

"And are you walking now, slowly, hand in hand?"

"Oh, yes, Ruth, we are. And it's so great . . . to be hand in hand with Jesus . . ."

"Now, in your imagination, Jeff, you walk each step of that entire distance to the barn door."

After a long pause, Jeff said, "We're there. We're locking the door."

"Now turn around, and walk step by step, hand in hand, with Jesus back through the darkness to the house."

After some silence, Jeff said, "We're there."

"Now open the door and go back into the house."

"No, Ruth. I want to stay outside, in the dark—with Jesus."

After much laughter, and many tears, and many more comments about Jesus' power to heal, we talked about forgiveness being a key to emotional healing. I asked Jeff if he saw any need for healing in his past relationship with his mother.

"Ruth, I just don't see it. But I have that Alka-Seltzer stomach feeling that *you* think I do."

"It doesn't matter if I do or don't, Jeff, It's your life, and your insights are what matter. Would you like to experiment for a moment?"

He was still smiling broadly as I asked him to close his eyes and go back to about his fifteenth or sixteenth year and find himself somewhere in the home where he lived at that time.

"Still our old farm. My bedroom," he said.

"Bring your mother into your room."

"Dr. Jekyll's there."

"Good. Now see if there are any cords connecting you to your mother."

"Oh, my Lord, what's this all about? I do see them. They're all over me. I feel like I'm waltzing with an octopus! I'm serious. It feels awful."

"Jeff, imagine Jesus appearing in your room."

"He's here."

"See a golden sword in his hand. He'll give it to you."

"O.K. I've got it."

"Now take that sword and cut those cords. Cut them all. Don't let one remain connected."

Jeff went through a pantomime. He held an invisible sword in his two hands and swung vigorously.[2] All the group was praying . . . all but Clifton who, gripping his closed Bible, watched with suspicious curiosity.

"I got 'em all," Jeff sighed.

"What do you see on your mother's face?"

"Disappointment," he said slowly. "Could Dr. Jekyll have been Mr. Hyde all along?"

"I don't think any such images are necessary, Jeff. She was an imperfect mother as all mothers are. Before you open your eyes, let me remind you that Jesus said, 'Whatsoever you loose on earth, you loose in heaven.' You're loosed from any cords of control from your mother. He also said, 'Whosoever's sins you forgive, will be forgiven.' So, if you choose, forgive her."

He opened his eyes. "I'll forgive her, but I want to know something from you, Ruth. When I felt those cords around me, was that my inner child, all tied up? Was that child singing 'I love you truly, Mother' when I should have sung 'Mother, I want to be free'?"

"Your inner child has wanted, Jeff, to be free all along. Because you had repressed memories, you just didn't know what, or who, was binding you. As the cords were cut, you were being set free from the bondage of your mother's overprotective love. Your child's song of love is true and broke through to freedom from the depths of your heart. The healing took place."

"Now I see," he said, "why Marceen's constant pushing and controlling drove me out of my tree. I had married another mother."

"That's a different subject that will take a lot more discussion. But I think you're on to something."

Jeff couldn't adequately relate to a woman. The tip-off clue had been that he couldn't even kneel before one comfortably until those threatening, smothering, choking cords were cut away.

Parent and any child beyond puberty would do well to see if there are cords binding the inner child. There can be no true maturity in relationships when "smother love" binds the human spirit.

Frequently, when one seeks to discover cords in a faith-imagination relationship, it is helpful to imagine them ever so faintly, then to ask oneself, "If I could see them, where would they be attached between my parent and me?" Sometimes, if they are a subconscious reality, they will appear and remain. If there is no subconscious substance to the cords, no parental overcontrol, the imagined cords will either fade or never appear.

Where cords have been connected in childhood and now become severed, it is helpful to examine other dependency relationships to see if emotional cords have been formed between the self and any other significant person—a spouse, teacher, boss, minister, or, most especially, one's own children.

One of the basic principles of inner healing is that this exercise of "cutting the emotional cord" has to be repeated. Growth requires time, and repeated reinforcement of the new positive pattern forms habit. The instruction of the Scriptures "cast down imagination" (2 Cor. 10:5) and "whatsoever things are true . . . think on these things" (Phil. 4:8) and "make love your aim" (1 Cor. 14:1, paraphrased) all imply constant reinforcement, the habit of cutting cords, repeated action until the mind-set of maturity, Christ's mind, is permanently yours.

But removing a negative image by "cutting cords" is never enough. It's only a "half-job" like removing the old chicken coop from your backyard. It's still desirable to go on and build your dream house.

After Jeff's cords were cut, he had to learn to use each successive negative experience with a woman as an opportunity to forgive and build.

Forgiveness lies at the heart of all inner healing. This is being obedient to Jesus' instruction, "Love your enemies." In many cases, "Private Enemy Number One" is one's self. Self-forgiveness is essential to self-healing. And each time you forgive another, your own sense of self-forgiveness and self-worth will grow. It is the surest way to improve your own self-image. But it is also a powerful means of developing that master male or female image within, which Jungian therapy calls the *animos* (the male image) and the *anima* (the female image).

Let us imagine that a man has been reared by an overcontrolling aggressive woman, one of a myriad of variations on Jeff's experience. One of the gravitational principles, "like attracts like," seems to be a psychic economy of our universe: We draw to us the kind of situation we most fear. Jeff's negative inner image of a woman invites painful encounters with aggressive, manipulative women. After the healing process begins, he must deal with each successive anger-hurt reaction as quickly as possible. He should get quiet and use faith-imagination to visualize his mother in some earlier overcontrolling situation. Love may be visualized without feeling it. An imagined Jesus can shine light on that mother or cast a healing light that can be seen entering her body. Creative imagination makes all things possible in a forgiving state of mind; healing love is being applied. He can then see his mother coming to be reconciled, each asking forgiveness of the other, then embracing. In this way, a habit-formed positive image replaces the negative.

A friend told me how she applied this method. She was standing in line at the ticket counter at a large municipal airport. A man walked up and placed his bags right beside her. Then, ignoring the line, he pushed in front of her and asked the agent for a ticket. She said to the ticket agent, "Excuse me. I was next."

The agent snapped, "Lady, wait your turn."

She felt a surge of tremendous anger. Realizing this was the reaction of her inner child, she moved out of line, sat down in a waiting area, and asked the Spirit of God to help her. Her mother's unfortunate tendency to treat her unfairly had been heard in the agent's unwitting mistreatment. With faith-imagination she "saw" her mother and prayed for her. The moment she did, peace poured in. She then prayed for the agent and for the inconsiderate man. As she returned to the line, she was thrilled with the victory. Her mother was more beautiful; she herself was more beautiful, and the whole world was a little better place because she took those few minutes to bless instead of curse.

In each faith-imagination replay, the image of the offending parent will grow more positive. You, in your mind, are allowing your parent to grow to his divine potential or perfection. What may begin as an ugly, undesirable image will, through this simple discipline, be transformed into that perfect image that God intends and that you must have to develop emotionally and spiritually to your full potential.

Variations on Jeff's experience with his mother are common to emotional problems in our society. Our social structure requires men to be married to their careers and allows them to fail at home. The employer who demands most of a man's time imposes a shotgun relationship upon unaware fathers. The mother is given an unnatural role— hybrid mother-father. The father is rarely present to provide the love-discipline relationship with the children for which he is best suited. In such a situation, overcontrol by the mother becomes easy. Its negative effect has been traced in detail. It creates emasculated men, social violence,[3] and an absence of male spiritual leadership in and out of the home. It has created a generation of women who feel uneasy sexually. They find the whole experience of sexual relationship clumsy or, worse, distasteful.[4]

Those of us who are parents, and who desire independent children, must constantly reexamine our parental need to control growing youth.

To release an adolescent is not to abdicate one's role as

parent. It is emotional recognition that your child's responsibility must increase and yours must decrease. Parents must allow an expanding number of significant decisions to be given to the child. This especially applies to the mother, who, naturally and correctly, has been in a strong directive role until the teen years. Parents must recognize the right of a youth to become an adult, to learn through experience and mistakes, even mistakes that are painful for the parent.

Those of us who know Jesus as Son of God and Savior sometimes find it difficult to understand that he is also Son of Man, our human ideal. To those who really want to follow him, he becomes a very human being who developed in his life as we ought to develop in ours. He "increased in wisdom and stature, and in favour with God and man" (Luke 2:52, KJV).

Profound inferences arise from Jesus' experience in the Temple at the age of twelve. A significant relational guidepost to all mothers and sons, this event marked the important transition between Jesus the boy and Jesus the man.

The family caravan was returning from the Passover celebration in Jerusalem to Jesus' childhood home in Nazareth. Joseph and Mary were certain that their responsible and obedient son would be with one of the families among the many in the travel group. They were wrong.

And they were upset when they found him missing. They were human, too! When at long last they finally discovered Jesus in the Temple, Mary reprimanded him: "Why have you done this?"

But Jesus did not apologize. "I thought you knew I would be about my Father's business." He had no reason to apologize. He had cut the cord. He, without rebellion, had returned to his home. But you may be sure that if Mary had not cooperated by "pondering in her heart" his new manhood under God, if she had tried to retard him by retying the apron string, his manhood would have been diminished and her motherhood marred.

Jesus and Mary, his mother, our examples, challenge us to be ready to cut the cord with our children when they reach their teens. To ignore this divine pattern is to endanger their emotional health.

4

NO PLACE TO HIDE

"When all kinds of trials and temptations crowd into your lives, my brothers, don't resent them as intruders, but welcome them as friends! Realize that they come to test your faith and to produce in you the quality of endurance" (James 1:2-3, Phillips).

Seated in my library, I had just finished my morning cup of coffee. I picked up the phone, and a man's voice said, "Mrs. Stapleton, you don't know me, but . . . my wife, Mrs. Joiner, is going to be placed in a mental hospital if she can't find help right away."

He was phoning from the freeway near my home where they had stopped on their way to seek more psychiatric help in another city and possible hospitalization for this troubled lady.

Within minutes after I had put the phone on the hook, they arrived at my door. Her face was taut with tension and fear—wrinkled brow, brittle smile, too-rapid speech. Following the formalities of greeting, she burst into tears.

"Oh, dear God, what is wrong with me?" she wept.

As she told her story, she used every possible sub-conscious tool to hide from herself. Much of her life had been a flight from reality, though it wasn't apparent to her as she spoke. She needed to escape, for her emotional scars were many and painful.

Her mother died when Mrs. Joiner was only four years old. She had no substitute mother-figure after that. A series of housekeepers did what they could. Daddy cared. He loved her when he was at home, took her places when he could. His only failure was that by himself he wasn't enough. He couldn't be mother and father both. No one parent can, no matter how well-meaning. She had been robbed blind emotionally while being raised in com-fortable affluence. As she began to move into adolescence and womanhood, two things began to poison Mrs. Joiner's relationships with everyone: her feeling of rejection from others, and a poor self-image as a woman. Every child needs a mother. She had none, and for a little child that amounts to rejection. Every little girl gets her image of womanhood from her mother. Where could Mrs. Joiner get hers? And almost every little girl thinks of her mother as the most beautiful woman in the world. Since Mrs. Joiner had no childhood image of a beautiful or an ugly woman, the void was inexpressibly painful.

Each of us can identify with Mrs. Joiner at one point. You and I have an imperfect self-image which was formed by our parents. Because no parent is perfect, mother and father invariably begin to feed ideas about manhood and womanhood that are less than perfect into our thinking and into our experience.

When mother and daddy express anger, or punish instead of giving understanding, feelings of guilt or anger develop where there should be self-respect. If either parent clings and smothers a child when love and freedom should be shown, the child begins to experience the loss of his warmth and spontaneity which is the beautiful quality of an emotionally healthy child. Such a child thus becomes self-conscious. Feeling manipulated, his or her tendency is to respond by trying to manipulate.

Most of us feel that we are less than the persons we should be. In reality we are wondrous creations of God, possessing infinite capacities for love and living. But these words sound like cheap pep talk until the negative material fed into us since before we were born is removed.

Mrs. Joiner avoided coming eyeball to eyeball with her poor self-image by one of the most popular escape tactics of our society. She got busy! Because her good mind was her point of strength, she joined the intellectual rat race. She taught in programs for the improvement of higher education. She became president of the local art guild, then, appropriately, a member of the mental health association. Obviously, there is nothing wrong with any of these activities, but Mrs. Joiner's subconscious motivation was wrong. Her frantic doing made her activities destructive; she was always too busy to face herself. Her escapes were benevolent and intellectual, but they were escapes, nonetheless.

To recognize need, to be willing to face the problem, is a first step to inner healing and spiritual awakening.

Mrs. Joiner had all her defenses well positioned for everything except radical surgery. As she lay in the hospital bed, she had no committee meetings, no stimulating conversations about art or education. Her pain and loneliness walked into a haunted house of past memories. Tears, depression, and uncontrollable anger toward her husband began. And when her calm, dignified mask slipped, she began to see that her worst problem was herself. But what caused her poor self-image, she did not know.

As the disparity between Mrs. Joiner's feelings and her relatively good circumstances widened, her pain grew. But still she wasn't through trying to deceive herself. Her next ploy was predictable. She began to look for a scapegoat—someone to blame! Hesitantly, with anxiety, she shared a secret episode of her life. Before she had married her husband, she had known an attractive young doctor. They had experienced more than a passing attraction.

One day, while seated in his inner office discussing a nagging throat condition, she suddenly "saw" him for the first time: his piercing azure blue eyes, strong chiseled features, dark, uncombed hair "that looked nice but not neat." His face flushed with the surge of unexpected warmth. She felt admiration and attraction more than passion, but she knew she desperately wanted him to hold her. Beginning to tremble, she hoped he would not notice her feelings, but he did. As she stood up to leave, he walked from behind his desk, took her two hands in his, and said, "Please know you're much more than a patient to me. Could I take you to dinner sometime?"

Clumsily she blurted, "I suppose you could."

She walked out into the waiting room wishing she had been more encouraging, more feminine, more something.

Two days later the doctor telephoned. They had dinner together, then several other dates. That was the summer she met her husband. A whirlwind romance and then marriage removed the doctor from the picture.

Now faced with emotional crisis, the warm memories of her old boyfriend, the doctor, became another reason for agony. Instead of facing her negative self-image, she discovered another escape hatch, another excuse, another "reason"—"If only I had waited for the doctor; if only I hadn't married Tom."

Her husband became the barrier between herself and happiness. And she constantly assaulted him with a barrage of criticism. He could do no right.

In a moment of weakness, she called the doctor. More than twenty years had passed but, yes, he remembered her well. They met for lunch the next day in a well-appointed restaurant. There was a lot of talk about the past. He had never married. After lunch there was a warm good-by, "It's been wonderful to see you again." Although she felt some guilt, this meeting fanned the flame of blame directed toward her husband.

She tried to space her calls to the doctor. She always guarded her feelings, but she was still grateful he made no physical advances. She knew how vulnerable she was yet recognized that she couldn't handle the guilt of an involved affair.

Two years later her crutch collapsed. The doctor had a

heart attack at the age of forty-eight on the fourth fairway of the country club golf course. A fellow physician tried to revive him, but every effort failed.

After the stunning effect of this news wore off, Mrs. Joiner began to realize that the doctor could not have been the answer to her problem. She was now more convinced than ever that her problem was herself. At last she was ready to seek help.

Mrs. Joiner's pattern of escape should ring personal bells. When we are unhappy, it is easy to pass the buck. We immediately want to blame our job, the boss, our spouse, a friend, finances, the government, our circumstances, for our misery. And it is usually not too hard to build a case against the situation or person that irritates us most.

Ultimately, external factors do not make one unhappy; they only expose the negative material within our own subconscious. Unless the negative material is eliminated and the subconscious condition corrected—healed—this exposure of the unhealed subconscious can lead to negative reactions. A woman goes blind and commits suicide. Yet, Helen Keller, both blind and deaf, was one of the most noble, happy persons to walk this earth. A man loses a son, exists under a cloud of bitterness, and never recovers. Yet, H. G. Spafford lost two sons in a shipwreck in the Atlantic and went on to Israel to found the Children's Hospital and the H. G. Spafford Foundation. He became a radiant human being. Why, between these extremes, are there so many different responses? Why do life's external circumstances and dark moments bring tragedy to one, triumph to another? Each response is the result of inner wholeness or brokenness, maturity or immaturity, healing or nonhealing.

Have you realized that the things which most upset and anger us in others generally involve our own areas of emotional weakness? Yet these same stumbling blocks "in others" can be the first stepping stones to our own healing when we understand the principle.

Saint Paul said, "You are inexcusable, old man, whoever you are when you judge others. For when you judge another you condemn yourself, you who judge, do the very things you are judging" (Rom. 2:1, paraphrased).

That is at the heart of most of our anger toward persons and life. *We lean on people most severely at the point where we ourselves are weakest.* One of the better ways to learn about our need for inner healing is to keep careful account of what angers us most deeply and most consistently and to note the reasons this occurs.

Mrs. Joiner had sought no spiritual help. Some pushy religious friends had tried to convince her that she needed "to be saved." Argument from these lapel-seizing, evangelistic types offended her intellect. They had composed a neat, sterile set of doctrines that didn't require emotional commitment and had adopted a position as "intellectual" as the intellectuals they scorn.

Mrs. Joiner, cold, calculating, impersonal, was utterly enraged by these religious dogmatists—cold, calculating, impersonal. Sterile intellectualism will always be offended by sterile intellectualized religion, but love can reach in and dissolve any reason for keeping God out.

As I listened to her express contempt for religion, I

prayed silently. How could this troubled spirit know at all
the love of the Jesus who said, "How often I would have
drawn you unto myself as a mother hen draws her chicks
under her wing?" (Luke 13:34, paraphrased). Mrs. Joiner's "inner child of the past" had lost her mother; the
mother hen's wings had folded in, chilled and stiff, and the
baby chick was left out in the cold. How could anyone be
expected to accept the love of Jesus when her child-heart
remained crushed? And how many, many other hearts are
there in this world who can't accept the love of Christ because life has dealt them such a bitter blow?

As Mrs. Joiner was finishing her story, I asked, "What
would you like to have more than anything else in life?"

Quick tears sprang to her eyes. "My mother's arms
around me," she whispered.

The beginning of her healing was to help her experience
a mother's tender, unconditional love. So through the miracle of the God-given ability of our minds to create, we
would try to reform her outer life by transforming her
inner life.

"Mrs. Joiner, please close your eyes," I requested. "I
want you to imagine yourself as a four-year-old child.
Remember where you lived; visualize the house itself. If
you can't recall it as it was, reconstruct it as you imagine
it to be."

The journey backward is usually difficult at first, but as
it becomes a game which obviously one cannot lose, the
mind relaxes. Then one can withdraw from the memory
bank of the deep mind the record of each moment of
one's life.

She couldn't recall the house vividly.

"That doesn't matter," I assured her.

She then began by creative imagination to form her childhood home.

"Now, see yourself as little Joyce in one of the rooms of the house."

We sat in silence as she imagined the scene. She found herself in her first home, in her bedroom. She saw a doll in her arms.

"I feel so lonely," she said.

Of course she would. Her mother's death was interpreted by her child-mind, the subconscious mind, as rejection. She had been told, "Your mama has gone to heaven," but they had showed her the still form of her mama in that box. Her mind flashed back to a funeral—the room, her living room, had flowers, too many flowers, and an awfully sweet smell. And that pretty box with mama in it. Lots of people hugged her and said sad things. She couldn't remember what was said. Most were crying when they spoke; so it must have been sad. She knew mama wasn't in heaven; she was in that box. They took her mother away in that box. She never had a mother again. Mama left her; Joyce felt rejected.

What Joyce Joiner didn't know was that on that day the facts of the funeral had cast a shadow over her whole life. As she grew up, these early moments of apparent maternal rejection had compelled her to expect rejection. Even when people liked her, she often felt that they didn't. Since rejection creates feelings of loneliness, Joyce was always lonely, even in the company of friends.

Often Jesus would say to the sick and emotionally

broken, "Your faith has made you whole," as though their faith had generated the miracle. And he was saying exactly that. It is the power of faith-imagination that does what is needed to bring healing.

"Little Joyce," I said, "as you stand near the box your mother is in, I want you to look toward the front door." I paused. "Do you see it?"

"Yes." Her adult face showed grief, but the tension was gone.

"Now, Joyce, see the door open and see Jesus walk into your house."

The mature Mrs. Joiner who considered herself above "religion" could not have done this. Her "adult" thinking had allowed Jesus to be a significant historic figure, maybe one of the most significant. But he certainly was not a Savior; she wanted nothing to do with such medieval ideas. Mrs. Joiner was accustomed to keeping everything under control through careful intellectualizing. What she was about to do, what she had to do to find healing and wholeness, is just what Jesus said was necessary. She had to let go and become as a little child.

Unlike Mrs. Joiner, little Joyce held no such opinions: "I see him!" There was excitement in her voice.

"What is he doing?" I probed.

"He's walking toward me. He has his arms out. He's kneeling down beside me."

"Let him embrace you." I didn't need to suggest this.

Mrs. Joiner, through tears of joy, said, "Oh, he already is."

Jesus was loving the child Joyce. And this love was an

event as real as the funeral in her childhood. Such faith-imagination has a very real effect and is basic to one's understanding of this healing method.

Maxwell Maltz said, "Something imagined vividly enough and in some detail is as influential on one's emotions as an objective event experienced." [1] Faith imagination creates an objective experience. It does not approximate or simulate one.

Mrs. Joiner's face was bathed in a warm smile. Beyond any theological or rational argument, she had met her Savior. The man who loved little children and blessed them had done it again.

But little Joyce's wish was still not realized. She had not yet felt her mother's arms around her.

"Joyce," I said, "let Jesus go to your mother where she is lying, and let him bring her to you alive. She is alive. Can you see him going to her?"

"Yes." Her voice was hushed. The smile was gone from her face.

"Where is your mother?" I asked.

"Still in the box."

No encouragement, no suggestion could bring her mother out of the casket. The damage was so deep, mother was so dead to Joyce, and all the rejections that followed in her life from this first and worst experience were so heavy that Joyce's mother seemed to be buried under forty feet of unrecognized pain.

"As is your faith . . ." Jesus had said. Well, Joyce's faith in mother was just not up to resurrecting her from the emotional grave.

Throughout Joyce's life it seemed that women had rejected her. Some rejections were real and some imagined. She remembered several women teachers who, when she had sought approval, had deliberately turned their backs on her. She worked harder than anyone else in the classroom, and she got excellent grades, but she felt herself a total failure because those teachers rejected her.

Job said, "That which I have greatly feared has come upon me" (Job 3:25, paraphrased). It usually does. No doubt, Joyce had consciously tried too hard to gain approval from women while sending out the subconscious, nonverbal signal that she expected to be snubbed. Begging for rejection, Joyce realized what she had greatly feared.

The sadder situations which developed, however, were the times when people really cared for Joyce. They offered their acceptance, but Joyce, governed by the fears and conditioning of her deep mind, could not believe acceptance. She felt that she wasn't really accepted. She interpreted the slightest criticism or complaint as rejection.

Joyce was at an impasse. She couldn't get her mother out of the casket. How, then, could she experience a mother's tender embrace?

Just as there are substitute, or adoptive, parents in the physical world, so there can be such substitutes in the life of the mind. My thought was, "What better substitute mother could Joyce find than Mary, the mother of Jesus?"

Picturing in my own mind the child, Joyce, standing before her mother's casket, I said, "Honey, let Jesus hold your hand."

"He's holding it," she responded.

"Now let him walk with you to your bedroom."

"I'm there."

"Walk in and stand with Jesus by your bed."

"He's lifting me up and sitting me on the edge of the bed."

"All right, now invite Mary, Jesus' mother, into your room."

I watched Mrs. Joiner's expression for any telltale emotion. Could she allow this most glorious of ladies to appear in her emotional world?

"She's standing there. She's standing in the doorway," Joyce sounded awed and apprehensive. "She's so beautiful."

"What does Mary look like?"

"She's dressed in soft, sky blue—a long dress or gown. She has a sort of shawl over her head. Her face—she's so lovely. And she's smiling at me."

"Can you let her come to you?"

"Yes, she's coming."

There was a pause, and then Mrs. Joiner broke into deep, wracking sobs. She could barely speak through the flood of emotion.

"Holding me, holding me, Mary is holding me."

I moved beside her on the sofa where she was sitting. I put my arms around her and let her put her head on my shoulder. When the emotion was spent, she began to open her eyes.

"Close your eyes for a little longer. We have one more thing to experience." As she closed her eyes, I said, "Go with Mary into your living room. Jesus is leading the way."

"I'm there." Then she added, "It's so much brighter in the room now. I can see details. The mirror over the fireplace. The green and gold draperies on the front window."

"Now, Joyce, let Jesus go touch your mother. Let him bring your mother to you."

"I don't know what's happening. There's my mother; I think it's my mother. It looks like pictures I've seen of her. And the box, I mean the coffin, is gone."

"Let your mother come to you, Joyce; let her put her arms around you."

"She's just standing there," she indicated. There was still some fear, but very little. "She's smiling at me."

"Joyce, ask Mary to bring your mother to you."

Mrs. Joiner put her head back on the couch where she was sitting. As the child, Joyce, she lifted her arms. In the eternal now she reached up to her mother. Mrs. Joiner was weeping. Over and over again she repeated, "Oh, mother . . . oh, mother . . . oh, mother . . ."

Her deepest desire had been fulfilled. Her mother's arms held her at last.

5

IS HEALING OF THE MEMORIES
SCRIPTURAL?

"This above all: rely upon the words! Words are the safe, sure passageway into the Temple of Certainty" (Mephistopheles' Advice to Student, Goethe's Faust).

"Ye shall know them by their fruits" (Matt. 7:16, KJV).

"This woman is a witch disguised as an angel of light." I couldn't believe my ears. He meant me! He went on: "I take authority in the name of Jesus Christ to stop this meeting."

He couldn't *do* this; I was in charge. I was standing in front of more than sixty women, all seated, all listening, leading them in prayer—a deeply tender devotional which attempted to direct their imaginations creatively to certain inner emotional areas where they could be healed, could allow repressed memories to surface and painful ones to be touched by Our Lord.

The minister glowered. He pointed a long, accusing

finger at me. He meant business. Unmistakably, he intended to stop this meeting, to clear the hall, to keep these women from listening to what he characterized as heresy, or blasphemy, or anathema, or whatever "good Christians" shouldn't listen to.

Me—a witch? Salem, Spanish Inquisitions, auto-da-fé— a thousand grisly histories avalanched into my mind.

The place wasn't twelfth-century Madrid or seventeenth-century Salem or reformation Holland or Geneva or Bloody Mary's England; it was Longbranch, Alabama, 1970. I had been asked to lead a group of fashionable, intelligent women ranging in age from twenty to sixty—mostly in the thirty- to forty-year age range. We had been in intensive teaching sessions of memory healing for two and one-half days.

An hour before this Christian minister's dramatic entrance, he had stalked into our meeting place, the guest house of a private home, and had interrupted with incredible accusations that I was "unscriptural," "unchristian," and "demonic." He had denounced me as a false prophet.

I had listened patiently and then responded: "I am in charge here. You have not been invited. I have been asked to pray with, and love, these people in the name of Jesus Christ. You, sir, are out of order. You are not in charge of this program, this place, this meeting, or these people. They have been entrusted to my care and the care of the Holy Spirit. I, therefore, ask you to leave . . . now."

He had left. I thought I had disposed of the threat. But now he was back because as minister of one of the nearby country churches he felt that "his" flock of sheep were there and needed protection from me—a "theological wolf," heretic, blasphemer, and witch.

On this second visit, he demanded that every woman leave the meeting and that every other scheduled meeting be canceled. Some women protested, others broke into tears, some pleaded with him, but every woman walked out except Sally Jones. When I walked out, I reached for the minister's hand. His hands stayed rigid, frozen to his upper thighs.

I said, "I may find out some day that you are right about some of the things that you said and that I have been wrong. Or I may find that I am right and you are wrong. But one thing I know, for sure, now, is that the way you have handled this situation is the most un-Christlike exhibition I have ever experienced in my life."

Sally Jones, who stood by me, took me out to lunch. Then we went to my hostess's house to pick up my luggage. Another woman, who was to offer her home for the night meeting, called and said her husband was not a Christian, but that when she related to him what had happened at the morning meeting, he had said, "No one says who can, or cannot, come to my house to speak. Invite her."

I agreed to go. The husband, a young doctor, invited many of his close professional friends and their wives. This meeting lasted until 2:00 A.M. and was a success.

The group who was to sponsor me the next day for a luncheon called to say that they had voted as to whether or not they would allow me to speak on Friday morning. Since the luncheon was by reservation and was prescheduled, they felt they should go ahead but warned me that they would be scattered throughout the room and I was not to speak on anything other than salvation.

At the luncheon the next day, six extra tables had to be set because word had spread concerning "the witch." The television station and newspapers had sent reporters. When I was introduced, I apologized that my horns and tail weren't visible for exhibition at that particular time, but that there was salvation for them anyway. After the successful luncheon, I was immediately escorted to the plane.

Subsequent close touch with Sally Jones informed me that there was a town revival after I left. They played my tapes over and over and wrote down every book I mentioned, read them, and studied each Scripture, every reference.

About six months later, the minister sent his apologies. I sent word back that reconciliation was not possible until he was willing to stand publicly with me in Longbranch before the people whom he had confused and apologize to them. I have not heard from him since.

Attacks similar to these have been leveled against me. I have had speaking engagements where twenty churches canceled upon the charges that "Ruth is a false prophet teaching doctrines that are unscriptural" (meaning inner healing). Sometimes this charge is combined with others: "She is a woman, leaving home to teach elsewhere; she is not submissive to her husband." (Many hold the idea that most ministers of inner healing are women.) One of these occasions was clarified by the chance meeting of a prominent minister and one of the girls who had worked for me typing manuscripts. She answered many of his questions:

"Does her husband object to her work?"

"No. He is the one who is most supportive."

"How do the children react?" "They, too, encourage her. They feel that, if they have need of her, she puts them first."

Most of the criticism that my ministry of inner healing has received seemed to be concentrated into one fall afternoon when an imposing, sincere, fundamentalist minister requested an interview. His questions, doubts, fears, included most of the orthodox charges that have been hurled at me.

"Mrs. Stapleton," his voice was gentle, but edged with iron, "I have come to see you in the name of Jesus Christ. I have heard many complimentary stories about what you have done to help people, but I'm not at all sure that my text for the day isn't 'Not all those who say "Lord, Lord" shall enter into the kingdom.' "

"We're starting upon solid mutual ground, reverend; I love the Scriptures, and I love our Lord Jesus Christ."

"I know others who love both—five ministers to be exact—who feel outraged by your use of his holy name and a ministry that has no parallel in Scriptures or in the mainstream of orthodox Christianity."

I remained silent. He continued: "Mrs. Stapleton, outrage can spring from gossip, hearsay, personal animosity, many irrelevant sources. We have already been blessed with our criteria: the Scriptures, a Counselor, the Holy Spirit, and a judge, our Father God. But before I go on, I want to be very sure of facts. Would you tell me in your own words just what you do? How does your ministry operate?"

I told him the stories of Mary Ann, Nick, and Mrs.

Joiner as I have related them in the first three chapters of this book.

"Mrs. Stapleton," his voice was grave and sober, "this sounds to me like psychotherapy, or psychoanalysis, or some mongrel bastard child of both. Are you a psychologist? Are you a psychotherapist? Do you have a psychology degree? Do you have the credentials to practice psychotherapy? Of any kind?"

"No, to all of those questions."

"Mrs. Stapleton, I don't let just any surgeon operate on my wife; I don't let just any dentist check my children's teeth. And yet any surgeon or dentist has had to pass rigid tests, board examinations. I would never permit a psychiatrist to operate psychically upon my wife or administer shock treatments or chemotherapy without checking thoroughly into his reputation. Even if the reputation is bad, the credentials are there, the competence to deal with emergencies has been passed upon objectively by legislative standards. Suppose that my wife came to you. Like Mary Ann or Mrs. Joiner, she has a memory so painful that she has repressed it. Through your counseling techniques, and I'm not sure I should dignify them by labeling them that, you expose the memory. It causes her such pain, such terror, that she goes into deep melancholia. This has been known to happen."

"Not in my experience, reverend."

"But if it did? How do you treat her? How do you get her out? Suppose she became so depressed that she took her own life? How would you feel about that? How could you undo the damage that you did?"

"Reverend, it seems to me that you have concluded

67

that I am a psychotherapist practicing without a license, that I operate psychically upon patients. Is this what your five minister friends have also concluded?"

"This is one of their conclusions."

"This is unfair. The facts that I have reported to you do not support any such interpretation. I am not going to defend myself against labels that aren't remotely related to facts."

"How so?"

"I don't need to defend myself against the charge of practicing psychotherapy or psychic surgery. I have never done either. I never intend to."

"What *do* you do, Mrs. Stapleton."

"I help people to find and expose repressed painful memories."

"Isn't that extremely dangerous?"

"Not when they arrive to confer with me. They consent to look for the memory with my help. This is an act of free will on their part, or upon the part of those interested people who bring the person. But, reverend, we do this only after prayer to our Lord Jesus Christ; we ask his divine blessing on the search. Do you believe that Jesus is Lord of all? Lord of the imagination? Lord of the subconscious? Lord of the repressed memory?"

"I do."

"Do you believe that even if asked, he will allow—in his holy name and service—a memory to surface that is too painful to be dealt with—*by his love?*"

"No, I don't."

"The repressed memory surfaces through his power. It

is then dealt with by his power. If any 'surgery' is done, he is the surgeon. All I do is attempt to bring the pain to light and then introduce that pain to Jesus within the imagination of the person I counsel. Is it scriptural to convert? Of course. Is it scriptural to evangelize? Of course. Is it scriptural to convert the will of another to the will of God as revealed in Jesus Christ? Of course. Is it scriptural to introduce our Lord into the heart? The emotions? Why not introduce him to one of the highest of human faculties —the imagination? What can the Lord Jesus do to your imagination if you let him in?"

"He is already in control of my life. I am saved. If I am saved, by definition, one of my faculties, my imagination, must also be saved."

"Suppose, hypothetically, that you suffered from an experience in your childhood that was so painful that you buried it in your subconscious. It was so terrifying that you could not face it at the time and never wanted to have to look at it again."

"If it's buried that deeply, how can it affect my life? Or my relationships?"

"The mental institutions are full of these people. Let me tell you of Mrs. Z., in and out of institutions for thirty years. They brought her to me. They expected me to pray for her and that Jesus would heal her. When I began to talk to her, I saw that she couldn't communicate. As I looked at her trancelike state, I saw why they considered her case hopeless. I took her down by the lake in the sunshine where we could drink in the deep, natural therapeutic effects of sun and water. We sat in the grass. While there,

I reached over and held her hand. She stared fixedly in a straight line. As I began to pray silently for her, I saw a stairway. If you don't mind, reverend, I'd like to take you through this prayer rather than just tell you about it. This is a great prayer if you can't speak the person's language. It does not require any response from the person. If he wants to respond, he can, but it can be used with people who cannot relate to me or to any significant other.

Lord Jesus, you are a part of each one of our lives; you know every moment we have ever lived, both the good moments and the bad. And so, Lord Jesus, I join with you and picture each of our lives as a staircase, a narrow staircase. It is going up. This staircase is lit with a bright light. Jesus, you are the way, the truth, and the light; you are the life. We acknowledge that each step represents one year of growth in our lives. Jesus, as you stand at the base of the step, we see ourselves as a little baby. We are there at the bottom of the stairs. Take that little baby that we are into your arms. As you hold us, as you rock that little baby, we thank you that your healing love begins to pour through into our hurting heart. All of the memories of that time that we spent in our mother's womb—all the hurts, all negative emotions that were picked up from outside—we ask you to heal. We thank you, Lord, that your light is cleansing and purifying and transforming all of the darkness within into light. And now, Jesus, walk up this stairway of life with us. As you walk, let your healing light remove all darkness in every moment that we have lived. We thank you for taking that little baby that we are and stepping up on that next step of life. Thank you, Jesus, for that first step and the healing. Now, as we step on that second step, we see you place that little child, that now can toddle, down on the step, and as you hold our hand, as we move up that stairway, we thank you that we are moving with you into perfect wholeness. Together we step onto the third step. And the fourth. Fifth, sixth. In the sixth year, as we begin to know the difference between boys and girls, and new confusions, the new traumatic changes that happen . . . we thank you, Jesus, that you are removing and healing all. As your light shines so brightly, we move onto the seventh step. Eighth. We thank you, Jesus, that we don't have to recall anything because we know that you are picking up things that need healing. We move to that ninth step, holding each other's hand; together we move on, ten, eleven, and so forth . . . And we thank you for your companionship through each year, Jesus. Amen.

"Reverend, I have done this with you just as I did with Mrs. Z. When I got to the twelfth step, Mrs. Z. began to scream. She remembered that at age twelve she had been raped by her father. She had never told any therapist. In over thirty years of psychiatric counseling, none had dug this out. Now with Jesus as her companion, in her consciousness, our Lord allowed it to come out.

"Reverend, *I* did not dig this out. *I* had never seen her before. I had no way of knowing, but the Holy Spirit did. He, in his mercy, brought it to the surface.

"Then, this woman, who couldn't communicate before, related all the facts to me. She relived them with much of the original pain and terror.

"Now, reverend, before we go on, a question for you. Did I do anything more than invite her into an exploratory search of memory with Jesus at her side?"

"I don't know. I wasn't there. From what you tell me, Mrs. Stapleton, you did not. You only prayed for recollection."

"Wrong. I did not pray for recollection; I asked Jesus to heal any painful memory of any year of her life. Anything that our Lord wanted to uncover was up to him. So far, reverend, have I committed psychosurgery? Without a license?"

"No, Mrs. Stapleton."

"All right. Now we come to more of the inexplicable, no explanation possible apart from Jesus Christ. I don't know of a rational hypothesis that has ever been formulated, by any humanist or scientist, that can account for what happened next. I took her back into those same terrifying memories, but this time, your Lord and my Lord was holding her hand."

"Mrs. Stapleton, don't tell me that you led this woman step by step through the traumatic details of forcible incest."

"No way, reverend, would I do that in her case. Some cases may require that, but she had already begun to talk. Already there seemed to be such a healing power present that I thought that the relationship with her father should be healed through forgiveness.

"I told her to imagine, or to sense, the presence of her father. She did. I then said to picture Jesus standing next to her father. She did. I then said, 'Jesus has his hand on your father's shoulder.' The fear that had shown in a convulsive muscular reaction when I told her to picture her father seemed to relax.

" 'Jesus is forgiving your father. Do you?' She slowly nodded her head, then spoke in a whisper: 'Oh, daddy, I forgive you too.'

"This is all I told her. Does this sound like psychosurgery?"

"No, Mrs. Stapleton."

"Am I probing into the subconscious depths with any scalpel except the Holy Spirit? Am I doing, have I said anything, anything that Jesus Christ would not have done had he been present—in your opinion?"

"Oh, I don't know about that. Aren't you being a little presumptuous? Don't you assume that you know without really knowing?"

"We both know, reverend, of Jesus' healing ministry. He healed wherever and whenever he could, in defiance of Sabbath, custom, Pharisees, and the establishment of his day. With this lady, in and out of institutions for thirty years, psychiatrically treated for thirty years, we have a repressed, inexpressibly tragic, painful memory exposed to the imagined person of Jesus Christ, the Great Healer. She is doing the imagining; I am not. She is consciously inviting the Holy Spirit to work in her memory and with her imagination. Jesus is in control—according to you—of both memory and imagination. I have suggested nothing but his healing presence. Reverend, what did I do? Psychosurgery? Did *I* probe at all? Who was the surgeon?"

"What happened, Mrs. Stapleton?"

"We left the lake to find her husband. Mrs. Z. was talking coherently, communicating sanely. Her husband could not believe first her communication, second her story. Then he wanted to take her back to her psychiatrists and the institution, but she wouldn't go. She insisted upon staying at the retreat until our meetings were over. She then told her grown children and later her psychiatrists. During the week of the retreat this woman ministered to others."

"An impressive story, Mrs. Stapleton, if you've told

me all the facts. And, *if* you do no more than this type of prayer leading in other cases. Are you sure there are no hypnotic suggestions or manipulative *techniques*"—he paused for emphasis—"I use the term respectfully now, that are employed?"

"The miracle, reverend, takes place in the conscious imagination of the person healed. The manipulation, if any, is that of Our Lord Jesus—his Holy Spirit—'manipulating' to heal. The healing is his, not mine. The ministry is his, not mine. And when you've watched him work in this way, and in as many lives as I have, you become the one who is hypnotized by the beauty of his caring and loving and tenderness with his children."

"Mrs. Stapleton, I have several questions. Why does it seem necessary for the subject to relive the painful scene in some cases, but not in others? Who decides? Upon what criteria?"

"Perhaps another case, that of Mrs. X., would help to answer your question. When she came to me, she said that every night of her life since she was forty years old, she had screamed in her sleep with terrible nightmares. She said, 'Even like when I come to this retreat center, someone has to come with me. I cannot sleep in a room alone. I cannot be alone.' She connected her fears at forty to what had happened when she was four years old, an experience with a burglar.

"He had broken into their house in the middle of the night, had attacked her, and she had screamed. Her parents got up, and the burglar crawled under the bed. After they put the light on, they pulled the man out from under her bed. This was emotionally terrifying to a small child, and this memory had, since age four, ruined her rest and those who had to sleep in the same room with her. That burglar was still there under her bed. After this, reverend, our conversation proceeded along these lines."

RUTH: Well, have you prayed about this?

MRS. X.: Yes, I have prayed.

RUTH: I'd like to pray with you now as you picture yourself as you were when you were four years old; see yourself in the house where you lived, now in the room where this experience happened. Do you see the bed that you were in?

MRS. X.: I see the house, the room, the bed.

RUTH: All right, now see Jesus coming into your room, and he is love, he is perfect gentleness. And he comes over in love, and he sits on your bed, and he takes your hand. Imagine that he is holding your hand. Imagine that his love is just flowing into and through you. All of your fear is being absorbed into this perfect Love.

"And, you know, reverend, when the person can really begin to be childlike, he finds a key to the kingdom."

MRS. X.: I do feel his love; I feel his warmth.

RUTH: Feel all pain now being absorbed in this love. Jesus is not going to hurt you; he's the only person in the whole world that you can trust. Now, are you holding his hand?

MRS. X.: Yes!

RUTH: Now, hold his hand tightly. Do you know who's under the bed?

MRS. X.: Yes, I know.

RUTH: We're going to have him come out. All right? Are you ready for him to come out? You know that Jesus is with you and nothing is going to happen to you? Now see this burglar come out from under the bed.

MRS. X.: I see him. He's coming out . . . (We were silent for awhile. Suddenly she began to cry.)

I paused, looked directly at my companion. I said, "Are you ready, reverend?"

He smiled sternly and said gently, "I don't know."

MRS. X.: Ruth, do you know what happened?

RUTH: No, what happened?

MRS. X.: Jesus told me to go wake my mother and tell her to set the table with the best crystal and china and to fix a feast because we had an honored guest. So I saw myself get up and wake mother up, and I saw the whole table loaded with all of the wonderful food. Then Jesus walked in. Do you know where he placed that burglar? At the head of the table, as the honored guest. He loves him as much as, if not more than, any of us.

RUTH: Isn't it wonderful. That burglar is a human being, isn't he? He's not a thing; he's not a frightful experience; he's a human-being-that-Jesus-loves. Mrs. X., can you love him with Jesus' love?

MRS. X.: Yes.

RUTH: Do you forgive him?

MRS. X.: Oh, yes.

RUTH: All right, you tell him. This is important, Mrs. X., to speak out verbally. Look right straight at that burglar and tell him, "I forgive you for all of the fear that you caused in me."

"And she did. Mrs. X. is crying. And so, by now, am I.

"Reverend, I couldn't have dreamed this one up. I couldn't have invented it by myself. Mrs. X. said these words to me, not out of shock and fear, but out of a creative imagination that sees a painful situation through the eyes of Jesus, the mind of Christ. Does this sound 'scriptural' to you, reverend?"

He remained contemplatively silent.

"In this healing ministry, reverend, I never know what the Holy Spirit, in the creative imagination of another, is going to do next, but I do know that when he gets into a painful memory, when he touches it, he heals it.

"Five nights later, Mrs. X. told the entire group the results of our healing prayers. Mrs. X. had not had another screaming night; she had slept peacefully and deeply, without fear, for as long as I was in contact with her. There is no doubt in my mind that this was a complete healing by our Lord."

"All right, Mrs. Stapleton. I'm willing to relinquish the charge of practicing psychiatry without a license. I'm willing, even, to report back to my five ministerial friends that you do not 'practice a therapy' as such . . ."

"People are healed, reverend."

"But that leaves us with a question as to whether or not

you are practicing some unscriptural techniques. Do you know of any Scripture that gives you, or anyone else, permission to do as you have done?"

"Not specifically. Not literally."

"Then, you admit that there is no literal scriptural basis for this inner healing?"

"No more than that there's a literal scriptural basis for sodium pentathol, or antibiotics, heart transplants, root-canal procedures, or orthodontia. Where is the literal scriptural basis for Salk vaccine to prevent polio? All are used to help God heal, to prepare a way for God to do the healing. I don't know a reputable surgeon who ever claimed that he did the healing; he only prepares the body for quicker and more effective healing. I don't claim to heal; I only try to prepare the person to be receptive for the healing in order that any unhealed, crippling memory can be touched by the Great Healer. And, as you can see, from what happened to the lives of Mary Ann, Nick, Mrs. Joiner, Mrs. Z., Mrs. X., their lives have been transformed. And I am always interested in the fact that each one of these people, except Nick, was a committed Christian before the transformation."

"Let us stay on the point, Mrs. Stapleton. If it's not scriptural, it cannot be Christian. If it's not Christian, you become a false prophet. Do you know of any Scripture that relates a story similar to the ones you have told me?"

"Yes, I do. Jesus' dealing with Simon Peter. Jesus saw a weakness in Peter that Peter had yet to discover. Jesus knew that Peter would deny him. After Peter's denial of his Lord, the memory of this denial could have crippled

Peter psychologically for the rest of his life. What the emotional reasons were for Peter's denial are not recorded. It could have been rooted in feelings of inferiority that had caused him to brag to Jesus, 'I would lay down my life for you'; and then to proceed to refuse to be identified with this 'social outcast.'

"Two memories, Peter's boast and the three denials, needed healing. And Jesus proceeded to heal both. He applied three distinct therapies.

"First, Jesus reconstructed the moment of infamy as a moment of faith and love. Every present-day healing of a memory requires the memory to be fully unblocked. Some memories can be unblocked and healed without recall. If recalled, they can be relived constructively in faith and love. Any minister of healing would describe this as erasing the negative memory with a present, positive, spiritual, parallel experience. This is exactly what the Bible records.

"John 18:18 says that Peter was standing by a 'charcoal fire' when he denied Jesus three times. That is the first negative moment. John 21 records that as Peter and some of the other disciples were out fishing, Jesus appeared on the beach having prepared a 'charcoal fire' (John 21:9). Now, the only times the words *charcoal fire* are used in the New Testament are in these two places, when Peter denies Jesus and when Peter plunges into the sea to get to Jesus on the beach. But should someone say 'coincidence,' note what follows. Therapy number two, another distinct action: Immediately, Jesus asks Peter three times, 'Simon bar Jonah, do you love me?' (John 21:15–17). Three denials before a charcoal fire erased by three affirmations before a charcoal fire. That is what we seek to do in healing of negative memories today. This second memory healing method, verbal erasure of the negative and affirmation of the new positive, is constantly used today.

"But the healing process continues in Peter. You will recall that I suggested to you that God's grace to save is immediate and complete but that his work to heal and mature our spirits may continue as a process. 'Work out your salvation with fear and trembling,' wrote St. Paul (Phil. 2:12). That 'salvation' that Paul speaks about is not the work of the cross. The work and the result of the cross is final and complete. The 'salvation' to which Paul here refers is the process of developing our hearts so that we may accept and appropriate what Jesus has already made available by his finished work on the cross.

"The continuing process of emotional-spiritual healing in Peter is found in his dream experience on the rooftop in Joppa (Acts 10:9 ff.). This dream experience is the third type of memory-healing known to this necessary ministry of healing.

"I know a newspaper editor who was meeting with a group of Christians for a weekend retreat. He said he had no faith. He felt 'outside' this circle of Christians. The leader was a Spirit-filled man who understood the symbolism of dreams. The editor volunteered that he had had a disturbing, recurring dream. It was out of his actual experience as an officer in World War II, just as Peter's dream was out of his Jewish dietary experience. The editor dreamt about a moment when in Italy the Germans almost overran his position. The only difference was that in his dream the editor's gun was shooting Ping-Pong balls which did nothing to stop the enemy.

"The group leader was able, through this dream, to point out that his relationship with his father was negative and needed healing. The man's father had died when he was five years old. The group prayed with him that Jesus might be Father and Father-image to this fine but broken man.

"To this day, that editor confesses that the dream interpretation and prayer that followed was the beginning of his faith and a new sense of his manhood.

"Surely, reverend, no such 'good fruit' could come from a 'bad tree.' Only someone who had never seen such a healing moment, or who had never seen the blessings in Christ that followed, could condemn this type of healing ministry as 'unscriptural.' And, in light of the description of Simon Peter's memory healing, who but those who prejudge this ministry could brand it as 'unscriptural'?

"To me, a practice or belief can be 'scriptural' if it's in harmony with the Spirit and with the teachings of Jesus. *When a new action is introduced into the world by the Holy Spirit, there may be no specific Scripture to support the specific action. But there will be much in Scripture to support the Spirit and the result of the action.*

"For instance, nothing specific in the Word of God provided a precedent for Jesus' healing on the Sabbath. But he could point to the Law which allowed an animal to be lifted out of a pit on the Sabbath (Luke 14:5; Deut. 22:4). The clear inference is, if an animal can be helped on the Sabbath, surely a man, created in God's image, can.

81

Again, St. Paul shocked the church, which was rooted in Judaism, with his insistence that a man did not need to be circumcised to be saved. He had no specific scriptural support. But when he wrote to the church at Rome, he could point to the fact that Abraham was given the covenant of blessing of God when he was not circumcised (Rom. 4:9–12)."

"I am not persuaded, Mrs. Stapleton."

"I have not tried to convince you of anything, reverend. You came to me, to try to persuade me that I was not acting 'scripturally'—a far more gentlemanly approach than some have made. I believe that anything which specifically contradicts the teachings of our Lord, or the way he acted, or the spirit in which he historically acted, is unscriptural. I find nothing in this inner healing ministry that contradicts teaching, acts, or spirit."

"But, Mrs. Stapleton, I find no authority for what you do anywhere, in spite of the inferences which you claim in the charcoal fire repetitions."

"Do you find authority, reverend, in the results of the lives of those healed? Can you find it in your heart to acknowledge increased church attendance, increased participation, and greater financial contributions, sudden tithing, along with the far more increased loving attitudes, and more fruitful relationships, as being 'scriptural'? If you do not believe my stories . . ."

"I do."

". . . or if you disagree with my theory, or my theology, or my inferences, can you believe the acts and the fruits of the Spirit?"

"But how do I know that these fruits are of God unless they are literally authorized by Scripture? Not all those, even you, Mrs. Stapleton, who say 'Lord, Lord' shall enter . . ."

"Which, reverend, brings us full circle. This is the text you came with . . ." I let my voice trail off.

"I am not quite where I was when I came, Mrs. Stapleton. Nor, on the other hand, am I convinced by the fruits you claim."

"Thank you for your concern and your visit. I am convinced that these works are of God. I intend to continue to do what he gives me to do as long as he continues to validate and empower."

6

EXORCISM
OR INNER HEALING?

It was not easy for me to sit in this church. The adamant attitudes of the minister's message made me uneasy. I heard him point a verbal finger at each one in the congregation for harboring a demon. My long battle had been to help people see they were not necessarily victimized by some demonic force just because they had uncontrollable habits and violent emotions. Often I had argued that many uncontrollable attitudes or excessive negatives were caused by a need for the touch of Christ's love to soothe and heal deep-seated hurts and pains caused by unpleasant experiences. Now I found myself a captive audience to one who took the absolute view—anger is an attack of the evil one, smoking and drinking are the products of a demonic force and call for exorcism. Sleeplessness is reason to cast out the spirit of insomnia.

Horrors! I was terribly agitated, but the sermon had at last come to an end.

Exorcism or Inner Healing?

Two hundred people were hushed into palpable silence. Nobody moved. For forty minutes every one had listened to Reverend Victor Ironstone preach exorcism, demonology, internal affliction, and obsession. He had concluded by saying: "And now, I invite any one of you to come forward to this altar to receive the blessings of relief by exorcism. Anyone who feels that he or she is afflicted or possessed, or obsessed, or victimized by any uncontrollable impulse can be freed, in the name of Jesus Christ. You can be liberated from the demon you are carrying, freed from the curse of fear, insecurities, frustration, loneliness, or guilt."

No one moved. Victor kept looking—to left, to right, front and back. The silence became uncomfortable.

And as they remained motionless, I, sitting uncomfortably in the very last row, was bombarded by a kaleidoscope of unhappy memories. Victor had been invited, along with me, to be the "other main speaker" at this conference on healing. Instead of a complementary, supportive, joint ministry, Victor had spent most of the week attacking my teaching, my lectures, or my counseling. I had experienced difficulty adjusting to the subtlety and the comprehensiveness of his attack. To me, there had never been any necessary antagonism between exorcism on one hand and "creative imagination" or the use of faith-imagination for inner healing on the other. But Victor had leveled big guns at the ministry of inner healing. He had claimed that exorcism was biblical; inner faith healing was not. "Demons were scriptural, exorcism was scriptural; but the healing of painful memories—repressed or conscious—was not."

85

Now Victor had invited all to come forward to have their "demons" exorcised. I thought his invitation too comprehensive, too intimidating, too broad, for scriptural support. It seemed to me that "uncontrollable impulses" could be psychic light years away from demon possession. But Victor had made his invitation purposely broad to include those who, without conscious knowledge, may have been possessed by demons.

Still, no one moved. Was Victor a failure? Had he failed in his own eyes?

All of a sudden something was happening to me. I had to go to that altar. But, no! I would not! Why should I? What was causing this compulsion to stand up and move forward when it was against what I felt to be true teaching.

In spite of my negative reactions to his approach, I began to forget everything except my need for healing in certain negative areas of my life. I had experienced the process of healing as a gradual evolution toward wholeness, but if the process could be speeded through the ministry of this man, I had to be willing and welcome the opportunity. My thought was "wholeness at any cost," but for me, in the back row, walking to that altar might be too high a price. It might damage my previous counseling, or my ministry, or diminish my effectiveness for those at this meeting who looked to me for guidance in spiritual growth.

I decided, quickly, to let the Spirit protect my reputation. My heart moved toward the altar. And I, target of Victor's unnecessary antagonisms, felt that my feet must follow.

I stood, in the last row, then walked silently, steadily, slowly down the center aisle toward Victor.

I watched Victor as I approached, and I knew that all of the antagonism we had felt toward each other melted in that moment. We became one in Spirit and in purpose.

Before any were aware that I had made the first move, Victor spoke: "And, let me say, that if I were out there with you, and not up here, I'd be the first one to this altar . . ."

As he spoke, my anxieties and fears were washed away by the love and tenderness which showed in his words.

Then one person stood and followed another. Then groups. The entire audience rose and came forward.

Victor was a "success." He led all in a prayer to exorcise any and all demons present.

Except nothing occurred to corroborate Victor's lurid predictions of what could happen when demons were exorcised, when demons "made their exit from the afflicted bodies"—wretching, vomiting, convulsions, screams, groans, and so on.

After this, Victor's messages lost their overpowering, come-on-too-strong aggressiveness. They took on a loving, intimate, personal quality that had been absent.

Two days later, as the conference closed, Victor came to me, asking to learn all he could about inner healing of the memories. We decided that there is need for both ministries, that there could be difficulty in diagnosing which method of healing should be employed because the symptoms could be similar.

Victor and I began to disagree when he claimed that

all uncontrollable impulses indicate the presence of the demonic and, therefore, the need for the rite of exorcism. I claimed that I had seen hundreds of cases of uncontrolled lives where the person to be cured is controlled by the inner, crippled child within, where no demon possession is indicated.

I tried to point out that inner healing should always be tried first. I based this upon experiences in which people have come for inner healing after exorcism has failed. In many of these cases, failure of the attempted exorcism seemed to have aggravated the person's problems.

When a person has been the subject of such prayer and the pain or uncontrolled attitudes remain unrelieved, he or she is apt to develop more pain through the inability to respond. In turn this increases feelings of unworthiness and adds more guilt. When one feels beyond relief, one begins to feel then that even God cannot help.

A further danger of exorcism may lie in another direction: "I am no longer responsible for my uncontrollables, or my deficiencies, because I am the helpless victim of a demon."

A definitive treatment of the differences between the two healing approaches can be found in *Healing*, a book by the Reverend Francis MacNutt, O.P. Father MacNutt points out the uses of both approaches and the compelling reasons why, for careful diagnosis, healers should be acquainted with the symptoms of both. There should be no conflict between the two branches of healing; people working with exorcism and inner healing should be able to work together side by side.

For instance, one of the common cover-ups for inner pain is escape through the use of religious projects. Doing religious projects that act as cushions and blinders can keep one from seeing and feeling one's true needs. Jesus didn't use the rite of exorcism on the Pharisees, and it might be interesting to see how the rite might work if one wanted to cast out the demon of "overreligiousness." Jesus denounced the religious leaders of his day for their busyness, for they were not being honest about their inner needs. "You are white-washed sepulchres; Mr. Cleans on the outside, ugly and dead on the inside" (Matt. 23:27, paraphrased). Jesus didn't say this to be mean; he wanted to shock them out of doing all that "bad" good which kept them from a realistic view of their problems.

Furthermore, Jesus used many methods other than exorcism. He said, "Out of the abundance of the heart, the mouth speaks." In the Old Testament it is written, "As a man thinks in his heart, so is he." Jesus has been called the "constant contemporary" because he is always up-to-date as his insights on life are interpreted for each generation. His profound perception is so knowledgeable we can only hope to move toward it. Our insights are obscure, infantile. He was infinitely versatile. *Our tools are dull. He used a touch, a word, a look, spittle, mud, water, silence, as he probed into the "heart" to heal the human spirit.* All of these methods speak eloquently to the inner child and to the subconscious. They say little or nothing to the adult rational mind. Jesus said, "Those things which proceed out of the mouth come forth from the heart; and they defile the man. For out of the heart proceeds evil . . ." He seemed to be as concerned with the external symptoms as with their subconscious roots.

The subconscious is like a little child. It is sensitive, teachable, a mimic of the adult world where it lives. It has also been likened to a computer because it feeds back with uncanny precision the kind of material programed into it through past experiences. Computer scientists coined the word *gigo* to describe how a computer produces. It means "Garbage In, Garbage Out." If garbage has been fed into the subconscious, garbage is going to emerge. The need is neither to condemn the bad output nor to exorcise it. The need is to reprogram the subconscious. This requires discovery of where the programming is wrong, erasure of memories and the negative material they contain, and then replacement in that area of mind with positive material. The new material should be in harmony with the love revealed by Jesus Christ.

Inner healing is a ladder, not a single rung; a process, rarely a one-time event.

7

THERE IS A SOLUTION
FOR EVERY PROBLEM

"Neither do I condemn you" (John 8:11, RSV).

There was a knock at my door. Jane, a close and trusted friend, in a tone of voice that mingled distress and embarrassment, asked: "Ruth, can homosexuality be healed through prayer?"

My answer came after a tray of cookies and tea had been prepared and we had moved into the library.

"Jane, I don't understand this, but in the past two years, it seems that the largest part of my counseling has been in the area of sexual problems and, offhand, I'd say about eight or nine were homosexual."

"Well, praise the Lord! I knew you could help. A young man I have known through my business came to me late last night. He said I was the only one he could trust, and then he told me he was a homosexual. I told him I knew no way to help other than to pray; so I prayed for him. He really appreciated the prayer, but then he began to tell me of his life, and I didn't know what to do except listen."

"Jane, listening is one of the greatest tools of inner healing. So don't think you were inadequate. Did he tell you anything about his childhood?"

"Quite a bit, but it seems foolish for me to try to tell you about it. It was so involved. After he finished, I told him I knew about you and that you might be able to counsel with him. Would you please?"

Jody arrived right on schedule. Handsome, twenty-two years old, warm, intense, and not at all "effeminate," he moved right to the point. "I'm really miserable," he said. "Can you help me?"

When a person is really seeking help, half the battle is won. We didn't waste time because I knew Jody meant business.

Jody went on to share his religious faith, or lack of it. "Mrs. Stapleton, the first thing you ought to know, I'm not a real Christian."

"What do you mean by that, Jody?"

"Well, what I mean is, I don't know Jesus. I've been a church member all my life, but I can't really say Jesus has ever meant anything to me. I don't know if God will help us or if prayer will work."

My suspicion was that, since Jody was unable to identify with the most significant man in his childhood, his father, the man Jesus, or the Father, God, were subconsciously cut out of his life, too. Through past experience, I knew that if this were the case, it would be necessary for him to create a father image where there wasn't one. This can be done through faith-imagination. But, first, if possible, I felt he should deal with the guilt that saturates the attitudes of most active homosexuals.

"Jody, do you suffer much guilt over this situation?"

"I hated myself so much that I've threatened to take my life several times."

"Would you like to be free from the guilt, even if it meant you had to let Jesus do it?"

"Oh, I don't object to the guy. I just can't relate to any of the garbage I've heard. But I'll try. I'll do anything at this point."

"Close your eyes," I said. "It may be difficult to think of Jesus kneeling before you, but as you close your eyes, try to see him this way. If you can't picture him, sense his presence. That will be just as good.

"As he kneels before you, he looks into your eyes and deep into your life. He sees all that is within you. He knows every kind and good thing that you've ever done. He also knows the dark moments that are hidden even from yourself. He knows everything about you, all the unfulfilled desires and needs in your life. He loves you because of all that you are. He accepts you unconditionally! He knows that guilt that you feel deep within and your inability to express it, or to forgive yourself for it. He loves you with a perfect love as though you are the only human being in the world. His love is so strong that it is like a magnet drawing out all that is dark within you and you are set free.

"Now relax and allow his love to flow in and fill all the empty places. As he sends you love, it flows into every part of your being. You are being made complete. Imagine Jesus saying to you, 'Because I love you so much, I want you to love me.'

"Jesus rises to his feet and stands before you. He lifts you to your feet and turns your body so that you face him. Look into his eyes as he talks to you.

"He says that he wants to share his love. He says, 'I don't want you to have problems. I want to take everything upon myself. I want you to see how strong I am. Lean against me.'

"As you do, you find that he doesn't move at all. He is secure. Put all your weight against him. Let every care and burden fall on Jesus. Lean hard against him and feel that firmness. His love pulls you closer and closer. Let go and sense your body moving into his body. Your body merges a little more and suddenly you are standing where he was standing. This oneness is what he was longing for. 'I want you to be flesh of my flesh and bone of my bone. Where my heart beats, it is your heart. My mind is within your mind.' Every part of you has entered into Jesus. Nothing can separate you. You are one body in the Father. He will never leave you or forsake you. In your weakness, let go and his thoughts will come through. Jesus tells you, 'My Spirit will direct your path. If you'll let me, I will speak my words through your mouth. The kingdom of heaven will come on earth because of your willingness to be open to me.' "

Jody opened his eyes. He looked a little dazed—or puzzled. I told him to sit as long as he wanted, and I slipped out quietly so that he could be alone. When I returned, there was a stillness in the room.

"Wow!" he said. "I feel strange."

"That's a natural reaction, Jody. I think it would be well to go on home and have a quiet night. If you can come back next week, we'll talk some more."

Jody returned the following Monday night.

"How was your week?"

"Something is different. But," he quickly added, "I'm not over my problem. I still have these desires. But, Ruth, I've felt a strength I've never known before. And Jesus is very real to me. He's a real man."

"Yes, Jody. He's a real man! Do you feel you know him any better?"

"You won't believe this, but I've actually been reading in the Bible about him this week. He's like nothing else! I never thought of him, or heard of him, like what I read. What a man!"

I didn't dare discuss any religious terms with him. Not only had Jody identified intellectually with the historical Jesus, but he was experiencing the Spirit of Christ within. Now that he had a foundation, I felt it was time to hear his story. It was as I expected. His father had died when he was eight, and his mother had never remarried. During the period of time between ages nine and fourteen, when he normally would have shifted his interest and affection from his mother to his father, he had no father to whom he could shift his attentions.

In normal emotional development when a young boy

reaches the age of thirteen to sixteen, he begins to take an interest in girls again and shifts from the masculine attraction back to the feminine. Since this period of development was absent in Jody, it was obvious why men interested him more than women. His deep mind was still reaching out for a man, a father, that male affection God intended him to have, free from the overt sexual drive he now knew.

"Jody, did you date in high school?"

"No, not much. I tried it a few times, but I always enjoyed the boys more."

"When did you have your first homosexual experience?"

"Oh, about twelve or thirteen, I can't remember exactly. One of the older boys in school asked me to take a ride in his new car. Guess I was impressed. Anyway, that's when it started."

"Jody," I explained, "I'm going to do something that you might think is rather strange."

"Well, it can't be any stranger than last week."

"Just wait and see. I'll try to explain to you what I will do. I realize that when you were young you never had the experiences of going hunting and fishing with your dad. You never had the opportunity for the man-to-man talks that most boys have. But tonight we're going to take that memory bank of yours and build some great times that you'll never forget."

"How could this be possible? I can't go back into the past and do anything now. It's been quite some time since I was a kid, and I'm too big for kid stuff now."

"You're right, Jody. You and I can't go back; but Jesus

can. That's one of the miracles of his Spirit that we can't understand. With Jesus, time is not a factor. Don't try to understand, just trust me. With Jesus, every moment you ever lived or ever will live is a present-tense experience for him."

"Well, after last week, I'm sure glad I don't have to understand anything for it to work."

"Are you ready?"

"Ready." He sounded a little excited about his unknown venture.

"Jody, imagine that you are six years old. Get as clear a picture as you can of your sitting inside the house you lived in at the time. What do you see?"

"I don't really see anything, but I'm thinking of my old house, and I'm thinking I'm in the kitchen. Do I actually have to see it?"

"No, you're doing great. In faith-imagination you visualize with your thoughts. You're doing exactly right. Now, the doorbell rings. Go to the door and open it."

"Who's going to be there?" He sounded frightened at the realness of it.

"Jesus is going to be there. He's got a baseball bat and glove with him. He wants you to play ball with him. Open the door."

Jody, with eyes closed, slowly reached out his hand. "Does he really want to play ball with me?"

"Of course, he does," I answered. "Imagine now that you go to your room for your ball and glove and then join Jesus in the front yard."

Through the prayer of faith-imagination I slowly, verbally took six-year-old Jody through an entire ball game, strike by strike, hits, foul balls, errors, everything. Batting time alternated between Jody and Jesus in a setting that is duplicated ten million times a spring Saturday throughout the country. It was fun-filled but exhausting for both of us.

"What would you like to do now, Jody?"

"Go fishing," he replied with no hesitation.

We began again by moving Jody to age nine with the visualization of digging up worms. Step by step we prepared for the fishing trip, and off to the creek we went. Jody knew just the spot he wanted to go. Naturally, he caught the biggest fish, and the most, which pleased his fishing partner as it would any father. It isn't hard to imagine Jesus enjoying a day of good fishing.

Our prayers were over for another week. For the next few sessions, Jody experienced faith-imagination at various ages between nine and fourteen, building in experiences he had missed. The last session we had through visualization, he met a girl, experienced the normal excitement of a first date. He had a little trouble asking her for the date and picking her up, but the drive to the movie and stopping for ice cream sodas afterward seemed easier.

Jody was thrilled with the new life that had been building over the five weeks since we met.

"Is this the cure for any homosexual?" he asked.

"Unfortunately, no, Jody. We've prayed as if your problem was caused by the absence of a masculine image in your childhood. And all we've done is build within your memory bank, by faith-imagination, the necessary missing memories. With other homosexuals, the problem can be radically different. Some young men need to be healed of the image of the strong overcontrolling mother who gave the child a confused sense of manhood. Every person is different, and only by discernment, divine knowledge, and the guidance of the Holy Spirit can one know how to pray. With you, Jody, as with every other partner in every new prayer adventure, I try to be totally dependent on Jesus at all times."

"What about girls? Do they have the same type of problems?"

"Frequently, though roles are reversed. A strong feminine image is absent. I remember the last young lesbian I prayed with was healed when, during the prayer, she was able to recall a repressed memory from the age of six. Her father had caught her in the garage undressed with the little boy who lived next door. In a rage, he had beaten her severely with a rope he found hanging on the garage wall. For ten Sundays after, he kept her home from church and locked her in the dark garage. Can you believe that this father told his frightened little girl that this was God's punishment for sinning?"

"Oh, God, no!" Jody responded, overcome with empathy.

"Jody, I'm afraid this is not unusual. When dealing with sexual problems, I find too often that children have been overpunished by their parents when caught in common everyday child play of discovering their own bodies. Many parents do not seem to know that this is an expression of normal curiosity at this age. This sometimes destroys the desire for normal sexual activity and marriage. A young woman may abandon the idea of marriage while still consciously desiring a husband, home, and children. Too often, the cause is this kind of parental blindness."

"Ruth, do you think that this cause-and-effect concept can be found in every action no matter how bad it is?"

"Yes, I do. The more I experience in counseling, the more hesitant I would ever be to judge anyone again. As I see the bad memories, such as pain, loneliness, fear, and rejection, replaced by new, beautiful experiences, and scars of the past removed by Jesus' love, I know there is hope for everyone to be balanced and whole. We wouldn't have been told, 'Be anxious over nothing, but by prayer and thanksgiving let your requests be made known unto God' (Phil. 4:6) if he hadn't meant there was a way provided for peace and joy within, no matter how broken our condition."

"What's the greatest healing in the inner life of a person that you've experienced?" Jody asked.

Jody's question thrilled me because I knew what prompted it. As healing is realized, one begins to want to reach out to help and heal others. This is one of the surest evidences of growing health in mind, heart, and soul.

After thinking over his question, I had to admit I couldn't single out any one experience as "the greatest." The most recent is apt to seem the greatest. For Jody it seemed "right" to recall a recent encounter with Zeb, a twenty-one-year-old boy who had just been released from prison for the second time on conviction for exhibitionism.

"Yes, he was healed, but I must admit that was a tough one," I replied. "After spending almost an hour in prayer

and praise and seeking guidance, nothing had happened
to let me know the healing had occurred. Suddenly the idea
came to have Zeb visualize Jesus walking through each
room of his childhood home, filling it with his love and
light. When Zeb refused to go into the upstairs bathroom,
I knew we had the key to one of the locked doors of his
past. After much encouragement and with the assurance
that Jesus would walk in with him, together they opened
the door to that bathroom. Through sobs and mild hysteria,
Zeb told me his uncle had walked in on him many years
ago as he stood there masturbating for the first time.
Memories of his uncle's roars and cursing rebukes flooded
his mind in that moment. I repeated the words continu-
ously, 'Jesus, Jesus, Jesus,' throughout his story. As Zeb
began to regain his composure, he visualized Jesus there
in that room blessing him, blessing the room, blessing his
life, and most important, blessing the part of his body that
Zeb had so hated and had rejected. This last act, Zeb join-
ing with Jesus in blessing his body, was the act that
assured Zeb's healing."

Jody looked at me intently, in a manner which let me
know that I had been guided in telling him Zeb's story.
Then he stated: "You know, Ruth, maybe I'd better start
loving my body."

"One hundred percent right, Jody. You're well on the
road to total healing and maturity, but now you'll be in a
growth process by which you will break some old habit
patterns, former ways of thinking about yourself, and also
former patterns of where you go and what you do. You
may tend to fall back into some old immature routine, but

just remember, your strength comes from within. In any weakness you can depend on Jesus' strength. So don't hesitate to call on him. Keep in touch."

I last heard from Jody that he had dedicated his life to the healing ministry and that his healing was complete. As I think of him, I'm reminded how cruelly, thoughtlessly we treat the sexual deviant. He is called "queer" or "gay." He is neither. All deviants are needy, broken products of emotional poverty. They certainly aren't "gay." In one study of homosexuality, a member of the homosexual community in San Francisco said, "Show me a happy homosexual, and I'll show you a gay corpse." They need neither condemnation from the Establishment nor to be confined to homosexual societies where the problem is perpetuated and aggravated. They need our love, plus more searching self-knowledge, plus the opportunity to meet the Christ who loves homosexuals and who died to give them life and wholeness, just as he did for the "less condemned, just-as-guilty, respectable" people.

8

BORN TO SERVE

"If any man wants to be first, he must be last and servant of all" (Mark 9:35, Phillips).

Manuel, a young physician in Portugal, claimed to be an atheist. He had been reared by his mother alone. Manuel's unseen boyhood hero was an uncle in America who had become educated and "made good" in the new world. When Manuel, as a young psychiatrist, finally met his uncle, the uncle spoke of God, of Jesus Christ as his Savior. Manuel was shocked. "Please don't ever mention religion again," he told his uncle.

After he returned to his home in America, the uncle received a letter from his nephew which said, "You need never write to me again, and just cross Manuel out of your life. Forget me."

The uncle replied, "I'll not write if this is your desire. But my love for you will never let me cut you out of my heart."

Unknown to both Manuel and his uncle, a healing of

Manuel's deep mind had begun in their first conversation. That inner healing had to precede any significant experience that Manuel could have with God because Jesus had called God our "Father." Can you imagine the emotions of anger, rejection, and loneliness the word *father* had induced in the heart of the young psychiatrist? Manuel had never known a father and thought of his uncle as a surrogate or substitute father. Naturally, a surrogate would reject him too. When this didn't happen, healing upon deep levels began to take place. Later, when Manuel struggled in the darkness of subsequent emotional breakdown, he became conscious of this unrecognized deeper healing.

"In the darkness all I could cling to was you," he wrote to his uncle, "and the promise that you could never reject me. Then I sensed the power of Christ's love, the love you had told me about. And I knew it was true."

In the beginning, the Spirit may bring into your life just one person for you. This person loves you in a way that no one has ever loved you before. He loves you when you are at your best, but he also loves you when you're at your worst. He even loves you when you hurt him. This is unconditional love because it is not dependent on anything that you say or do. He loves you because you're you and for no other reason. This is the kind of love that Jesus brings to the world today, and it will be Jesus that has given your friend this kind of love for you. However, it is more than just your friend loving you with Jesus' love. That love has become so much a part of him that he is loving you with his own love.

Thousands of alcoholics have found sobriety through

Alcoholics Anonymous. They know how necessary unconditional acceptance was to their release from bondage.
Absence of condemnation opens the door to the miracle.
The transformation begins in a room where everyone knows
the dark secrets and shameful past because any transformed alcoholic has lived in that same shame and darkness. Alcoholics freely and openly share their feelings and
their past antisocial actions. To them, there can be no
suggestion that someone is unacceptable. Reformed alcoholics are uniquely prepared to serve other alcoholics.
They can "reach down" to pick up another unhealed drunk
without ever appearing to have stooped.

The deepest healing comes through persons who have
moved beyond condemnation, beyond forgiveness, into unconditional acceptance. As Maxwell Maltz [1] has indicated,
one can only forgive what he has first judged and condemned. We might add that we can only accept what we
have forgiven. And we can only be accepting if we have
given up judgmental attitudes.

Jesus didn't treat the fallen woman as a guilty person
who needed forgiveness. His response to her was, "I don't
condemn you." Had Jesus said, "I forgive you," she might
have inferred that he had judged her. This, in turn, could
have prevented her experiencing the pure love needed to
achieve the deepest healing of the heart.

Each of us, like this woman, like Manuel, like uncontrolled alcoholics, has this need for unconditional love.
Before the broken spirit can be made whole, one must experience unconditional acceptance.

As Jesus' unconditional acceptance opened the door of

105

a woman's heart to the kingdom of God's love, just so he opened my heart. In my walk from emotional distress into a new sense of stability and balance and purpose, one of the most important stepping stones was knowing not only that I was forgiven, but that I was acceptable. Forgiveness is necessary wherever there is guilt and condemnation, but if someone had come to me with even the intimation that I needed to be forgiven—for my failure as a mother, or my inadequacy as a wife, or my inconsistency as a Christian—I would have been devastated, not reformed! It was only as I sensed that there were those who unconditionally accepted me that I could begin to face my needs and find healing.

When I recognized what had happened to me through the acceptance of other people, I realized that I too wanted totally to accept others. This meant that I had to give up any judgmental attitudes that I found within myself, and there were many.

My repressed, and unhealed, and unrecognized guilts had made me judgmental and pharisaical. But I found one conscious possible release by refusing to accuse others. This helped me to stop excusing myself, which in turn forced me to look into my interior life to face my guilts. St. Paul helped me to see that the condemnation I laid so heavily on those around was actually an indictment against myself.

St. Paul said, with amazing emotional insight. "You are inexcusable, old man, whosoever you are who judges for wherein you judge another you condemn yourself. For you who judge do the very thing you condemn" (Rom. 2:1, paraphrased). This is always true.

To stand in judgment of another is to place ourselves above our brother, a way of rationalizing our resistance to the demand to love one another, to be a servant to another. Sometimes I seem to be saying, "That person does not need my services. I myself will determine who has need of my time." This is a form of pride, and yet the other side of the coin reveals another barrier to servanthood. "I can't serve. I'm not worthy. I still have unhealed areas in myself."

Which escape from our Lord's command to love, to servanthood, suits you better: Too good to serve others? Not worthy enough?

Either "escape" is pride—the cornerstone of the vices, the basis of all sin—which always must increase the hidden sense of guilt because in feeling guilty we are forced to retreat further into ourselves and separate ourselves from our fellowman. Pride is the barrier of self which thwarts, distorts, warps, and destroys the perfect love to which Christ calls and bids us to come. I cannot get out of the center of my universe unless I can put Christ in the center. *He* must be there if I am to be whole.

When I recognized the deadly pride involved in my many refusals to love and to serve, I was led to another spiritual truth. I willed to love; I willed to serve. Regardless of my opinions as to whether or not I was worthy, I found myself attracted to, and being involved in, situations where (1) I had been healed through the unconditional love of other people, and because I was healed could minister effectively to unhealed others, or (2) I needed healing in some area of my deep emotional life where my blind spot had not permitted me to know what was wrong. Where I needed healing, I found myself involved with others who had been healed and who could offer me their healing ministrations. Both areas required the ministry of the Holy Spirit. Both areas required me to be a minister of healing, or to be ministered to. When I saw this universal principle of attraction, sort of a "spiritual gravitation," I was able to bypass the prideful "judgmentals" that had barred me from servanthood and had sinfully shut Christ and his Holy Spirit out of potential healing situations.

Circumstances have compelled me to recognize that I have drawn to myself from within my inner being any situation or person needed for me to grow and respond according to the principles of Jesus' teaching perfect love. If there is a negative area within, it will draw to itself a comparable negative within an experience or person. This confrontation of negative with negative often appears to be a test, a trial, or a temptation. "A man must not say when he is tempted, 'God is tempting me.' For God cannot be tempted by evil, and does not himself tempt anyone. No, a man's temptation is due to the pull of his own inward desires, which can be enormously attractive" (Jas. 1:13–14, Phillips). Much depends upon our response to that trial. We can either react negatively or we can respond according to Jesus' teachings by returning good for evil, loving our enemies, and turning the other cheek. There is no right response to any person or situation except to love. When we react negatively, no healing occurs, and we continue to feed the negative within us. When we have reached the place of responding in love rather than reacting negatively, we have come to love and totally accept ourselves. Then we will be able to love and accept our brother with the same love God intends us to have for ourselves.

Sometimes this principle of the "attraction of likes" is clarified by our reactions, our personal attitudes toward another. How do we respond to situations which call for our forgiveness of another? Jesus calls us to avoid judgment and to be ready to forgive as often as forgiveness is needed. Yet, we all know how hard it is to achieve this forgiving spirit. I find it the most difficult to achieve when the wrong I am asked to forgive is one to which I have felt a strong reaction. Perhaps I have never been willing to face this reaction for what it is, but within my heart is the telltale, vague, and disturbing sense of guilt. When Jesus said, "Love your brother as yourself," he knew this would be possible only by forgiving and accepting ourselves. Some of these areas we don't know about and can't even begin to see or face.

The underlying truth may be that when we bitterly react it is usually to those who are weak in the same areas we are weak. A person who has lived with liars and hasn't dealt with lying patterns and their consequent guilt finds other liars contemptible. A thief cannot forgive a thief. We often cover our own weaknesses with rationalizations: Gossips don't feel that they gossip; they just "privately share" with everybody in town.

When we can't forgive another, we are actually facing an overt expression of our own guilt in that person. This is one of the meanings behind Jesus' warning at the end of the Lord's Prayer—"If you don't forgive, you won't be forgiven." The implication of Jesus' words is if we refuse to forgive another, it's because we haven't forgiven ourselves and consequently can't experience forgiveness. But it is obvious that a God of perfect love has forgiven us before we even ask. Our block is that we are unable to receive his forgiving love because of our inability to forgive ourselves. Remember the picture Jesus painted of God in his story of the Prodigal Son, the total acceptance, the total forgiveness of the father who runs to greet his returning son.

Guilt acknowledged in ourselves, or in others, may be released through an experience of unconditional love and forgiveness. Such forgiveness can be experienced in everything from the ancient church sacraments of confession and absolution, to the words of Christ from the lips of the most lowly child. "I don't condemn you."

When we can say with our whole being, "I don't condemn you," while seeing another's imperfection, we are ready to be an instrument for the healing of mind and soul. When I resolved to love and to serve without being judgmental, when I resolved to love unconditionally, I found another exciting fact of life in Christ: Situation after situation allowed me to help heal or be healed. This is why each person has a unique contribution to make to the healing ministry. And it is recognized, at last, as one's own part in a thrilling purpose whose scope the finite mind can only glimpse in high moments.

What may be difficult to understand is that frequently our own lives are mirrored in our surroundings. Each of us has drawn to ourselves situations and people with similar needs and dependencies.

My willingness to serve comes through yielding to Christ within the situation that I find myself. In learning to yield comes my inner healing, a new sense of wholeness—the discovery of a treasure that every fiber of my being calls me to share with others.

Born to serve? Yes! Lately I have come to understand that this gives meaning to my life. It is the one purpose which can give a sense of fulfillment and joy. But to enter upon or even stumble into this awareness, we must humble ourselves, as did our Lord, and find the same obedience to his call as Jesus exemplified in his earthly life and ministry. My awareness of my call to serve intensifies as never before my need for greater growth. Never have I had a deeper desire to be more Christ-like, more real. And never have I been more sure that the writer to the Hebrews was speaking to me when he said, "A stumbling foot on the right path will never fail."

I don't want to be known as a religionist; I just want to know Jesus in the situation where I find myself. I have no desire to be a noted speaker or preacher; I just want to share him with others. I have now learned that I was born to serve because living his life is living service. I particularly want to serve those who are broken as I was broken and be served by those who have been broken as I still need to be broken.

Since healing is an ongoing process, it will have begun before we have even heard the terms *inner healing* or *healing of the memories,* and it will continue long after we have prayed specific prayers for inner healing.

To the degree that we are healed, that same healing is made available to all those in our lives who have bound us in any way or that we have held in bondage—to our parents, our children, our mates, everyone that our lives touch. We will then have become a tiny part of that vast and infinite love which reached out tender arms to every human soul, which yearns for the enfoldment of all within the completion of the family circle in a radiant realm of joy beyond description.

To the degree that we are healed, we will draw to us those in whom we recognize a need, a hunger; those who can be served because they know, at last, a sense of their own need and are ready to admit it to themselves. And we will also draw unto ourselves those who have begun to discover the hidden meaning of their own lives and feel the throbbing within their spiritual veins of the great electric current of God's infinite love. We are somehow able to recognize in each other our common Source, our Universal Father, our mysterious kinship, our incompleteness. And in our incompleteness is our wholeness; this is our inner healing. All of our incompleteness, all of our negatives, are completed and made positive in our willingness to admit them and to serve under the Lordship of Jesus Christ.

This is the ball game that you can't possibly lose: I serve you; you serve me; we're all in it together. We have found ourselves, at last, in the new kingdom. And in the joyousness of homecoming, we sink together to our knees, lifting up our souls to the source of our joy as naturally as the flower unfolds its petals to the sun, and prayer will flow from within us as freely an breezes blow and clouds drift across a summer sky. The music of the soul will sing itself in prayers of praise and thanksgiving. We will know a feeling of having been cleansed, for guilt and penance and confession have now yielded to the healing power of love. And the cross has become a great, stark cathedral reaching upward and upward into the blinding beauty and radiance of that kingdom which he came to earth to reveal. In that blessed radiance, every painful memory is washed clean; we are revealed in our wholeness to others and to ourselves. And we discover that our wills are no longer ours. They have become his will, and there is no separateness. We are whole; we are *alive* at last!

NOTES

Chapter 3

1. The New Testament calls this the gift of knowledge, a capacity to tune in on the psychic life of another without conscious communication. Its value is in healing the inner child; its danger is that if revealed carelessly it may be too painful or too perplexing. It must be used with great care and love.

If the person cannot accept the knowledge, healing can be blocked. Jesus used this gift when he said to the woman at Jacob's well, "You speak the truth when you say you don't have a husband. You have had five husbands. And the man you are living with now is not your husband" (John 4:17–18, paraphrased). But often Jesus had insights and remained silent. He said of Nathaniel, "Here is a man in whom there is no guile" (John 1:47, paraphrased). That is all he said; he knew much more.

2. If the use of images such as a *sword, cutting,* and *octopus tentacles* seems excessively violent, unloving, or unscriptural, they can be very harmonious with New Testament instructions. As the Holy Spirit encountered the apostle Peter in a dream (Acts 10:10–13), he was instructed to "Rise, *kill,* and eat." The Word of God is described as a *sword* in several places.

St. Paul may have been inspired by God to use such imagery because of its power to touch such emotions, to instruct the heart. The *heart* is the part of our subconscious mind that motivates our action. The Scripture says, "As a man thinks in his heart, so is he." Abstract language and rational theories don't communicate as well to the subconscious as images and pictures do. Our Lord knew the value of pictured parables in counseling the troubled.

3. Charles Silberman, *Crisis in Black and White* (New York: Random House, 1964).

4. Marie N. Robinson, *Power of Sexual Surrender* (New York: Doubleday, 1959).

Notes

Chapter 4
   1. Maxwell Maltz, *Psycho-Cybernetics*

Chapter 8
   1. Maxwell Maltz, *Psycho-Cybernetics*